GIRL
BY BIRTH,
WOMAN
BY FIRE

The Get-Real Guide to Becoming
the Woman You're Meant to Be

Robin Goad

Girl by Birth, Woman by Fire
The Get-Real Guide to Becoming the Woman You're Meant to Be

Paperback ISBN: 978-1-967587-44-5
eBook ISBN: 978-1-967587-45-2

Design and cover art by Peaceful Profits.

To Macy, Carter, Graham, and Spencer

It wasn't always pretty, but it was always real.
I love you all more than I could ever possibly say.

To my husband, Shannon

I never would've had the courage to write this book
without your unwavering belief in me and your
unconditional love that always comes without
judgment. I am completely in love with you.
Thank you for being my rock and my heart.

This book is for women everywhere.

My heart's desire is that we can create a safe space
to be real with ourselves and others, so we can learn
from one another, grow together, and lift
each other higher.

TABLE OF CONTENTS

INTRODUCTION

The night my daughter went into labor, I didn't sleep.

My mind raced through everything Macy was about to experience: pain, exhaustion, and finally, after what I prayed would be a smooth delivery, gazing down in total awe of the sweet boy who made her "Mom."

I could anticipate what was coming for my daughter because I'd lived it myself. And while there are some things in life you can only *truly* understand by experiencing them firsthand, there's so much wisdom to gain from those who've walked the path before us.

That's why I kicked myself when I found out she was pregnant.

Of course, *What to Expect When You're Expecting* by Heidi Murkoff made its way to her nightstand, as it had mine when I was pregnant with her 29 years earlier. I didn't just read that book, I *devoured* it, really making it my own. I wrote all kinds of notes in the margins—my symptoms and remedies, cravings and favorite recipes, hospital bag packing lists, postpartum experiences—the raw, real stuff, as it happened to me.

Then, without thinking twice, I gave my copy to a friend with instructions to add her own notes and pay it forward.

But when I learned my first grandbaby was coming, I wished more than anything that I could give Macy that scribbled-in, decades-worn book. Imagine if she could get authentic lessons on pregnancy from the version of me who was freshly living it all.

Then I think about how much has happened since. I've gained thousands more insights not just on mothering but also on family, friendship, love, career, mental health, money, and then some. We have *What to Expect When You're Expecting* to guide us through the nine months of pregnancy, but where's the guidebook for the other 90 years of life? What can you reference when your marriage is hanging by a thread? When your friends scatter after college? When your career path stops making sense?

This big transition in my daughter's life kept bringing me back to these questions not just as a mom but also as a woman. I've raised four children, navigated two divorces and three abortions, reinvented myself and my relationship with God, and led a successful career in high-tech sales. I have done so much hard, healing work.

I longed for a way to share what I know to make the journey easier for other women. This thought reminded me of something I tried to do years ago.

Let's Get Real

Twenty years ago, I tried to start a small group for women in my church. I named it Let's Get Real. The idea was to get together and talk about the tough stuff most of us keep buried deep down in our daily lives. I thought people were craving that kind of truth-telling as much as I was.

So I set up my living room with snacks and a circle of comfortable chairs, and guess what? No one showed up!

I laughed it off, but if I'm honest, it hurt. It felt like the world was saying, "Keep your realness out of here." I didn't fully understand it then, but I was desperately seeking someone who could meet me in the hard places without flinching. I thought that if I shared who I was at my core, I might finally feel seen by others, and we could help each other navigate life's twists and turns.

I see now that "getting real" is a tall order. Many of us carry shame, doubt, and private struggles we assume others won't understand. But I still believe that so many women are hungry for that kind of connection because we're wired for it. We always have been.

For generations, women shared life's little instructions over kitchen tables in quilting circles, or while digging in the garden side by side. My maternal grandmother (Edna Earl, "Nanny" to me) and her mother (Lois "Ma" Blankenship) used to sit in a circle with their friends stitching blankets, shucking corn, or snapping peas by hand. It makes me blush to think that they were probably talking about *everything*: sex, raising kids, daily struggles, and complaints about their husbands.

Somewhere along the way, we lost some of that wisdom-sharing tradition. We've lost our villages. We don't make time to "get real" with each other like we used to. That's partially because we're busier than ever and also expected to be *more*.

These days, we're conquering the world in heels and power suits, or we're stay-at-home moms making sourdough from scratch and raising chickens with a kid on each hip. On top of these roles, we are expected to maintain fabulous homes, hobbies, marriages, and sex lives, and post about our thriving social circles on social media. Yet, despite all the advice out there, the real-life wisdom passed from woman to woman in honest conversation feels harder to come by.

That's why I wrote this book: to inspire more women to tell the truth so we can learn from each other instead of keeping our best insights bottled up.

I see my stories like bumpers at a bowling alley. Maybe they can help other women bounce back on track before landing in the gutter like I did. And if you've ever landed in the gutter, you know: Sometimes the only good thing to come from it is the lesson you learn. They're real. They're messy. But why hide them when they could lift other women up?

We don't need another self-help book telling us to try harder or be better. We're already drowning in that pressure. What we need are real conversations, real stories, and other women willing to lean in and say, "Here's how that went for me. Here's what I learned and what I'd do differently. I hope this helps."

How do I know we need this? Because now that I'm in my 50s, I keep hearing women say things like:

- If I could tell my younger self…
- I wish I could tell my 18-year-old self…
- I wish I could tell my 30-year-old self…

"I Wish I Would've Known"

Me? I wish I had known that after my 20s, my friends and I would scatter in different directions, and it'd take real commitment to keep in touch. I wish I'd known that putting just $50 a month into retirement savings when I was younger would have made an enormous difference by now. I wish I would've known that you should tell your boss if you're gunning for a promotion—or they might pass you up simply because they didn't know you wanted it.

We all look back on things we wish we'd known sooner. So why don't we do more to capture and share those lessons with each other? This isn't about avoiding mistakes or dwelling on regret. It's about getting honest, learning from each other, and turning our lived experiences into something useful for the next woman down the line.

For example, years ago, my boss gave me parenting advice that has stuck with me. He said, "At any given time, you are spinning five plates. Don't let the most important plate crash." And in the same breath, he reminded me, "No matter how busy life gets, don't miss the championship game."

When my daughter went into labor early, I was supposed to be in Washington, DC, for a major work trip. It was the beginning of the year planning cycle. Every leader on the team was sharing business plans for 2025. It's the one meeting a year you probably shouldn't miss. Executives were flying in from all over the world, and my boss expected me to be there.

That advice was tucked away in my mind, reminding me that showing up for the big moments matters more than anything.

So I sent a quick email: "I won't be joining you in DC. Change of plans. My daughter had a baby, and I'm needed at home."

Easiest decision and it was made easier with the help of a previous boss that has been preserved in my heart after all these years.

If I'm honest, I might not have made that same decision in my 20s or 30s. I saw my career as the most important plate I had spinning and prioritized meetings over field trips with my kids. But today, I have total clarity on what's most important. I know not to miss the big days.

What This Book Is Really About

Macy gave birth to my perfect first grandbaby as I started writing the first pages of this book. In the span of ten months, my oldest son got married, my middle son graduated from high school, and my youngest son will graduate from high school before this book is published.

Thirty years of my life have gone by in what feels like the blink of an eye.

I've felt a tug at my heart to help women for a few years now, but with all of these life changes upon me and time ticking by faster each day, I didn't want another season to come and go without taking the leap.

So I put together a book of lessons on womanhood that I wish I'd learned sooner, told through real, honest stories from my life. I've organized the book around the areas where women tend to wrestle and grow the most.

Here's how it's organized:

- **Part 1: Your Relationships**. The people we surround ourselves with influence so much of our lives. This section explores friendships, love, parenting, and the family dynamics that shape who we are.
- **Part 2: Your Career**. Next, we turn to work because we spend so much of our time doing it. We discuss what you thought you'd do, what you actually did, and what you might want next.
- **Part 3: Your Health**. Finally, we look inward. This section is about caring for your mental, spiritual, physical, and financial well-being.

As I've navigated the highs and lows of womanhood, I've found that getting real with yourself in these areas is crucial for becoming the woman you're meant to be.

When I spoke to my husband, Shannon, and my youngest son, Spencer, about the purpose of this book, I said it was to help women love the journey of life. Spencer asked what that meant, and Shannon explained, "You can't just love the home run. You have to love the practice and the process of getting better. If you only love the home run, you will never put in the hard work required to get the home run."

That's what this book is. Not showing off our home runs, but helping each other get more out of the process of living our most authentic lives. I hope the life lessons in this book spark conversations, deepen connections, and help you share your own lessons with the women in your life.

Let's build a community of women who want to move beyond the surface, choose depth over polish, and help each other feel less alone by being brave enough to tell the truth.

Here's to getting real and loving the journey,

Robin Goad

HOW TO READ THIS BOOK

Just like the copy of *What to Expect When You're Expecting* where I wrote my pregnancy experiences, this book isn't meant to sit on a shelf, pristine and untouched. It's meant to be lived in. Dog-eared and thumbed through. Scribbled in. Handed around rooms and passed down.

Each chapter weaves together personal stories, lessons, and insights I'd share if we were sitting in a women's circle drinking coffee (or maybe margaritas or wine!), laughing, and building our wisdom books together.

But this isn't just about my lessons. It's about yours too. At the end of each of the three parts of the book, I'll give you some questions to explore about your own life. These prompts are meant to help you capture your lessons, document your family's wisdom, and record the stories you want to be told for the ages.

I encourage you to keep a journal to write down what my stories bring up for you along the way, whether you jot down quick notes or pour your heart onto the page. This book is built for you to reflect, gather your best lessons, and let go of what you no longer need, so you can become the woman you're meant to be.

If you pair your reading with a journaling practice, the wisdom you gather may be totally different from mine, and that's great! This book can serve as a springboard to document what you wish you had known and what you learn along the way. Then you can make the most of what you've been through and share the love with your people.

Go ahead and grab a pen. Devour the pages. Make a mess of it. That's life, right? At the end of the day, I truly believe this is the essence of what we're here to do: learn, grow, and pass it on.

PART 1
Your Relationships

The best things in life and the biggest pains in the ass.

From the second you are born, relationships begin shaping your life, for better or worse. It's no wonder that the first time we meet our mothers, we're usually screaming!

Research shows that we form emotional bonds in the womb.[1] Relationships are our first human experience and the genesis of everything: how you love, how you fight, how you see yourself, and what you pursue. They are also the single most important ingredient in a healthy life, so naturally, they come with zero training.

Wouldn't it be great if we knew what we were walking into? Which friends were lifers, which partners were toxic, and which relationships would quietly drain the life out of us?

Not only do we not get a heads-up, but most of us also never really stop to ask if our relationships are actually good for us,

---

1 Noor de Waal et al., "Maternal-Infant Bonding and Partner Support During Pregnancy and Postpartum: Associations with Early Child Social-Emotional Development," Infant Behavior and Development 72 (2023): 101878, https://www.sciencedirect.com/science/article/pii/S0163638323000632?.

even the ones we've been in for years. Kids can grow up in horrible circumstances and think it's normal. You could be lucky enough to grow up in a good situation, only to get a rude awakening in adulthood that *that* isn't always the norm either.

Family, friends, and lovers can be lifelines or landmines— sometimes in the same week! So how do we build relationships that help us thrive rather than screw us up?

Part 1 of this book focuses on naming those patterns, getting honest about the relationships that shape your life, and deciding what to cherish and what to let go.

Taking the time to understand the truth about your relationships won't just help you make peace with the past; it's how you stop repeating it. Through reflection and maybe some unlearning, you can build the loving, meaningful, and mutually beneficial relationships you've always deserved.

CHAPTER 1

Family

Families should come with warning labels.

The first time I ever considered getting support for my mental health, I was 23. I was one year into my first marriage, and I already knew I'd made a mistake. I didn't want to stay married.

But as the good Southern Christian girl I was raised to be, I wasn't ready to admit that my heart knew this relationship wasn't working. I needed to demonstrate to my mom, grandmother, and everyone in my family that I was doing everything in my power to make the marriage work.

We went to marriage counseling (sometimes couple's sessions and sometimes individual sessions), and I actually learned a lot from Dr. Caldwell. (His advice wasn't all good but we'll get to that in chapter 3).

One of the first things he helped me realize was that two unhealthy people can't come together and expect to have a healthy marriage. News flash: if you and your spouse come from a dysfunctional family and neither of you has healed those wounds, you might end up replicating those patterns to create, you guessed it, a dysfunctional marriage. It sounds obvious, but that

> **NEWS FLASH: IF YOU AND YOUR SPOUSE COME FROM A DYSFUNCTIONAL FAMILY AND NEITHER OF YOU HAS HEALED THOSE WOUNDS, YOU MIGHT END UP REPLICATING THOSE PATTERNS TO CREATE, YOU GUESSED IT, A DYSFUNCTIONAL MARRIAGE.**

was a big realization for me back then. From there, I noticed therapy became less about my marriage and more about my past.

Inherited Patterns

As I opened up more in our one-on-one sessions, Dr. Caldwell began steering the conversation away from the issues between my husband and me and deeper into my family history. We discussed my childhood as an only child living with my mom and an abusive stepdad, and he asked about my grandmother's relationship history.

I remember thinking, *Wait, why are we talking about her? This is supposed to be marriage counseling. What does my family have to do with this?*

I didn't know it yet, but he was right. I grew up in a family where we never talked about emotions or any difficult topics. We pushed them down and kept going. That was normal in my generation, and it had everything to do with how *our* parents were raised.

If you look at the funny stories in your family, you can see how patterns are passed down. In mine, we'd always cut the ends off the ham before baking it. That's how my mom and grandmother did it, so we figured that must be how it's done. We traced it back after I finally asked why. My great-great-grandmother's pan was too small for a whole ham, so she trimmed the ends to make it fit. We'd been needlessly cutting the ends off the ham for 50 years!

When I started to really trace back the patterns showing up in my marriage, I realized many didn't stem from the relationship itself. They were inherited.

Wounds from the One Who Carried You

I volunteer to support women as they navigate postabortion healing. In that work, one truth surfaces again and again, and it never gets easier to sit with: as women and mothers, we are capable of inflicting some of the deepest wounds.

I hear story after story from girls still trying to make sense of the pain left by their mothers' words, silence, or absence, whether it was intended or not. And I've lived it myself. My mother never in a million years meant to teach me that I deserved to be mistreated by men. And I know I never intended to hurt or emotionally scar my children. Even with the best intentions, mothers can pass down wounds that we don't realize we haven't healed.

I had no idea that looking at the relationships in my family could provide insights into why my marriage was falling apart. No one ever told me the patterns that show up in your adult relationships come from somewhere and more often than not, that "somewhere" is your family.

Maybe you want to "fix" men because you saw the women in your family carry broken men on their backs like a badge of honor. Or you're drawn to friendships with dramatic arguments because that's what your childhood home was like. On a subconscious level, fighting feels more comfortable than anything else. You might think it's just "how you are" or "how relationships work." But often, these behaviors are echoes from your upbringing.

In my case, I ended up with a husband who mistreated me, partly because I thought that was normal. When I realized that my mom often tolerated poor treatment out of fear, not strength, it knocked the wind out of me. That was likely a survival mechanism based on what she saw growing up. Pain passed down from mother to daughter is often unconscious rather than intentional, but it continues to move through generations until we heal it. And we can't heal it until we see it.

My mom's story helped me understand my own. Her father died when she was 5 years old. No one told her that there might be a hole left in a little girl's heart, though she lost her father before she was old enough to fully understand. No one helped my mom realize that when her mother went to care for her dying husband, she might have internalized that as abandonment.

Because of that, she needed to feel in control of who walked in and out of her life, which showed up as the hot-and-cold relationship I saw her navigate with my stepdad.

As a child, it's impossible for your brain to comprehend how the same person who once protected your life has caused you pain. That's too much for a kid to understand, so it's up to us to process it in adulthood. If you don't acknowledge that heartbreak, you'll spend your life either replicating the pain or trying to outrun it. And you deserve a better story than that.

Family Is Where Your Story Begins

Before you ever made your first friend or went on your first date, your family gave you your first blueprint for what love is supposed to feel like. You learned the roles you needed to play in relationships to feel safe and accepted.

If you've never examined your blueprint before, you're not alone. If it took a brutal breakup or an emotional rock bottom for you to start noticing the patterns, I'm right there with you, sister! Most of us were never taught to think or ask: *Is this relationship healthy and beneficial for me, or is it just familiar?*

But if you want to change your story, you need to know how it started. You can't write a different ending if you're still working from a script someone else wrote for you. This isn't about blaming anyone; it's about finding the truth. It's worth taking an honest look at the patterns we inherited from our families of origin that may have helped us survive but won't help us grow. Because once you see the patterns, you get to choose which ones to nurture and which ones to pull up by the roots.

Looking back at my mom's story made me wonder about something bigger: Who set the tone for our family?

Who Set Your Family's Culture?

When you're a kid, you don't sit at the dinner table with your family and think: *Is this healthy? Is this a good model to follow?* You don't analyze whether your parents treat each other with respect. You don't question the tension between your mom and her sister, or wonder how your dad's relationship with his father affects the way he parents you.

You just absorb it all completely unfiltered: the way people talk, what they brush under the rug, how they handle big emotions, the ways they show they care. What you're absorbing, without even realizing it, is your family's culture.

Most of us think of "culture" as something tied to language, geography, or maybe your workplace, but families have cultures too. It's all of those unspoken rules, habits, roles, and behaviors passed down through generations that dictate what your "normal" is while growing up. Whether it's healthy or not, it shapes how you relate to yourself and everyone around you.

Have you ever stopped to ask who set the tone in your family?

Sometimes, it's obvious. If Grandpa is an old domineering man, the loudest and angriest person in the room, he probably ended up in charge. If he didn't have the emotional maturity to lead in a healthy way, his anger dictated how people communicated, what could be said, and who was expected to fall in line. No one said it out loud, but everyone knew: don't upset Grandpa.

The person setting the family culture should be healthy. They should be grounded, emotionally aware, and able to lead with care instead of fear. But often, the most dysregulated person ends up steering the ship. If you don't correct this, one broken family member can have a ripple effect throughout generations, creating a generational curse.

The kids learn from Grandpa that love sounds like yelling and that the only way to process emotions is to lash out at anyone who crosses their path. They may carry those patterns into adulthood and pass them on to their own kids and grandkids.

It could be Grandma, who grew up with a lot of trauma that she never had the chance to heal. Now, she lives in fear, which means she constantly tries to control everyone. It's out of love, but it comes from a broken place. Maybe it's Dad, who shuts down whenever emotions come up. Or Mom, who smiles through gritted teeth and insists everything is fine, even when it clearly isn't.

Because of my stepdad's violent outbursts, I became a master at reading the emotional weather in a room. I'd adjust my tone, my needs, and my facial expressions based on what I sensed other people could handle. My behavior changed too. I performed, achieved, and got involved with loads of activities because if I kept my stepdad busy enough, he wouldn't have time to go to the bar and drink. That would mean less yelling and fighting and more peace in our home.

When you grow up around people who make your world feel lonely, stressful, or unsafe, you end up bending yourself into all kinds of shapes to keep the peace, assimilate to the chaos, or simply to get noticed.

Do You Want to Please Them or Piss Them Off?

Many of us subconsciously replicate the behaviors we saw in our parents, but the way they parented us also had its own effect on our behavior. You may have tried to please your parents because they gave you more attention when you got straight A's. Or you may have swung in the complete opposite direction and rebelled against all their expectations and rules. Maybe you did that because you wanted to prove you were different from them, or maybe they gave you more attention when you got into trouble, even if it was negative attention.

Some of us spend our lives trying to please or piss off our parents, even as adults or when they are no longer around. I've done both. Some years I bent over backwards to be the golden girl, and other years I slammed doors and said, "I'm not like you."

Those choices come from a place of reactivity, not authenticity. True healing can't begin until we stop trying to prove something to the people who raised us and start asking what actually feels right for the lives we want to build.

For many of us, the most influential cultural shaper in the family is our mother. She's the one who gave us life, the one we look to for comfort, the one we expect to tell us the truth. When a mother carries unhealed pain, it can seep into her relationships, her parenting, and the way she speaks to herself. But when she's emotionally grounded and supported by healthy connections in her life, that stability becomes nourishment for everyone around her.

That's why I keep coming back to a concept I learned from nature. It changed how I think about our roles as women, nurturers, and leaders in our families.

The Mother Thread

You've probably heard the saying, "Life is about the journey, not the destination." But there's another layer to that: We can learn a lesson from plants.

Growth is hard work, but it's harder when we try to do it alone. Plants know this. Through a vast underground network, some plants share nutrients and send "distress signals" to one another when danger is near.

Scientists appropriately call the oldest, wisest trees Mother Trees. They act as hubs of wisdom for other trees in the forest. They share important nutrients and information to help younger trees adapt to environmental changes, improving their chances of survival.[2]

In that sense, life is about more than the journey. It's about the journeys of those around you and the vital information you can share with each other. That's why it's so important to know the history, connections, and emotional well-being of the people who helped you grow. Not everyone grows up in a healthy environment, but we should all do the work to spot the patterns and heal ourselves as best we can for the people who come after us.

---

2 Suzanne Simard, *Finding the Mother Tree: Discovering the Wisdom of the Forest* (New York: Alfred A. Knopf, 2021).

The forest has Mother Trees that pass down wisdom. Many of us were nurtured in an environment of secrets, silence, and survival tactics. We don't have to pass on what was given to us to the next generation. To leave a different legacy, sometimes you have to dig into the mess of your past and find what needs healing.

Processing Family Secrets

The good news is that it's never too late to heal. If you're ready to examine the patterns from your past so you can create a better future for yourself, I'll be honest with you: there's no easy way to start this process.

If you're anything like me, you don't call out for a life vest until you're drowning. You don't start asking questions until something in your life has broken down (in my case, my first marriage). For me to acknowledge that I had childhood wounds to heal, I had to hit a wall I couldn't climb over with hustle and prayer alone.

That's the one good thing about hitting a wall: It's an invitation to get real with yourself, and your family, so you can find healthier ways of navigating life.

If you're in a marriage that feels unhealthy, maybe it's time to ask your mom what the real relationship between her and your dad looked like. As kids, it wouldn't be appropriate for our parents to share everything. But as adults, we need to know. We need that context.

If you're not sure how to even pinpoint where you have healing work to do, start with your everyday frustrations. Say your husband walks through the door and slams it behind him. Something in you flinches, your heart starts racing, and it feels as if you've just been dropped into a fight you didn't sign up for. Maybe he didn't even mean to slam the door, but that's all it took for you to end up in a screaming match. Or every time you discuss money, your whole body tenses up, and you go into defense mode. It may feel impossible to have a calm, rational discussion about money and you're not totally sure why that is.

Here's the hard truth I learned:

When your emotional reaction is not proportional to the event that triggered it, that's not just a "bad day." That's a warning sign.

When a tiny match is lit and suddenly you're exploding like a can of gasoline, that's history talking. That's a pattern worth unpacking and healing.

Changing What You Didn't Choose

When you start digging, you might find patterns of control, fear, resentment, or silence that go back generations in your family. You might realize you've inherited more than your grandmother's cooking or your father's jawline. You've inherited their pain, their defense mechanisms, and the scars they tried to keep secret.

If no one else in your family has ever done this work, it's OK to be the first. You don't need their permission to seek the truth and start healing. My hope is that more women ask themselves this hard question sooner: *Do I want to repeat what I saw modeled, or do I want to build something better?*

Most of us never ask that question until our 20s, 30s, or later. We're knee-deep in habits that don't serve us, trying to survive adulthood

> DO I WANT TO REPEAT WHAT I SAW MODELED, OR DO I WANT TO BUILD SOMETHING BETTER?

in any way we can. It's hard to make space to get real with ourselves and face truths that we'd rather keep stuffed in the back of the closet.

But it's so important that we do.

You didn't choose the family you were born into. But you do get to choose the one you build next. That's where generational healing begins, and its ripple effect will reach farther than you'll ever know.

CHAPTER 2

Friendships and Community

Time, distance, and silence. If it survives those three, it's worth more than gold!

My grandmother had a knack for turning moments from her life into lessons for her grandkids. My favorite was the one about the chickens. When Nanny was a little girl, chickens were a means of survival. Her family, like many others, relied on eggs for both food and income. One night, a fox broke into her aunt's chicken house and killed all 12 chickens. At her young age, my grandmother could see that loss was devastating for a family of seven. But instead of feeling sorry for her aunt and cousins, Nanny went door to door telling her neighbors what happened and asked each of them for one chicken. Each neighbor said yes. By nightfall, my grandmother had rounded up 12 new chickens to replace the ones her aunt had lost.

Nanny didn't let the overwhelming task of replacing an entire coop of chickens stop her from doing her part. She knew she couldn't do everything, but if everyone in her world just did one thing, that'd make a big difference.

That's the power of community. Everyone has their one chicken to give.

Nanny leaned into her network and the spirit of shared responsibility that was common during that time to help a family member in need. That story reminds me of the phrase, "It takes a village."

But lately, I've found myself thinking, *Where has the village gone?*

Bringing Back the Village

During Nanny's childhood, it was natural to show up for neighbors. Women cooked, cleaned, grieved, laughed, and raised kids side by side. But somewhere along the way, many of us have stopped doing life together. The chicken-giving, casserole-bringing, checking-in-just-because kind of community has started to fade.

Today, we work harder, move faster, and fill our downtime with scrolling instead of real connection. But our need for community hasn't gone anywhere. If anything, it's more urgent than ever.

When you're about to leave your husband or have an affair, when your kids won't talk to you, or when there's just too much pressure to keep it all together, it won't be a miracle that saves you. It will be your friends. When life gets hard, you need girlfriends you can lean on.

My mom had two signs in our powder room that I saw every morning growing up. The first one said, "To be a friend takes time, and time is what no one has. Consider yourself blessed if you have one."

Isn't that the truth? And yet, friendships are the first thing to go when our plates get full.

The second sign said, "Never place a period where God puts a comma."

Are there any friendships where you placed a period when it should have been a comma? Any you ended too soon? Any you wrote off during a hard season when maybe they just needed a pause, not a goodbye?

Now's the time to find your "chicken." You don't need a packed social calendar to build a strong community of women around you. Just find one simple way you can make a difference in people's lives.

Your chicken might be to babysit for a friend, tutor your niece, or bake a dish for a neighbor. My chicken is often to donate or volunteer in my local community. Sometimes it's a simple text that says, "Hey. I'm thinking about you."

The world can be cruel. The foxes will come at night to steal from us. There are seasons when life doles out loss, hardship, and pure crap by the truckload. When that happens, you won't need a hundred people in your corner. You just need a handful of solid friends who have a positive impact on your life because their influence matters so much more than you think.

How Your Circle Shapes You

In chapter 1, we explored how influential family is in shaping our relationship patterns. But it's equally as important to pay attention to the friends we keep around. Maybe more because as adults, we get to choose our circle.

I've realized over the years that it's important to surround ourselves with people we want to be like. No matter how much about ourselves, the positive and negative traits of those around us can shape our beliefs, behaviors, and decisions. If we're not paying attention, we might end up surrounded by people whose influence goes against our values.

Say you start gossiping with coworkers to fit in. Before long, you notice that you enjoy it little too much. Or maybe a close friend always complains about money, so it's easier to convince yourself not to start that new business or plan that dream trip to Paris.

This phenomenon has played out in every social circle I've ever been a part of, and there's science to back it up. Studies show that financial habits like overspending or playing it safe can spread through social networks.[3] It can be as small as a friend convincing you to buy the purse you're eyeing at the store or as significant as the choices you make regarding home buying or saving for retirement.

Divorce can be contagious among friend groups. One study showed that a close friend divorcing can make you 75% more

---

[3] Sheza Riaz et al., "Influence of Financial Social Agents and Attitude Toward Money on Financial Literacy: The Mediating Role of Financial Self-Efficacy and Moderating Role of Mindfulness," SAGE Open, first published August 9, 2022, https://doi.org/10.1177/21582440221117140.

likely to do the same.[4] You might notice how contagious behaviors can be in areas like dietary choices, alcohol consumption, and exercise. Having one close friend shift their habits can influence yours, even if you don't live in the same house or city.

I have a people-watching game I like to play where I try to guess which couples are married in a group. For example, if a woman is wearing activewear, I bet she's married to the guy whose biceps are popping out of his shirt. I've noticed that married couples start to look alike, and so do friends.

Next time you're at an airport, watch how groups of people dress, act, and present themselves to the world. You'll see why it's important to surround yourself with people you'd be happy to have influence your life.

Think about the five people you spend the most time with. Do they energize you? Challenge you? Make you laugh? Inspire you to keep growing? Or do they leave you feeling drained, stuck, or small?

It's time to get real with yourself about your circle of friends and their impact on your world. Don't be afraid to reassess a person's purpose in your life. The sooner you recognize that friendships have specific purposes and that not everyone is meant to be in your life forever, the more hurt you can save yourself from in the long run.

---

[4] Rose McDermott, James H. Fowler, and Nicholas A. Christakis, "Breaking Up is Hard to Do, Unless Everyone Else is Doing it Too: Social Network Effects on Divorce in a Longitudinal Sample," October 18, 2009, revised October 7, 2013, https://papers.ssrn.com/sol3/papers.cfm?abstract_id=1490708.

Friendship Theater

Ever heard the quote, "People come into your life for a reason, a season, or a lifetime"? Not all friendships are created equal. Some people float into our lives for a short while, like leaves in the fall. They're light, easy, and enjoyable to be around for a season, but then they disappear when a patch of rough weather hits.

While a tree's leaves come and go, its roots grow stronger over time, keeping it grounded even in tough circumstances. We all need friendships like that to anchor us through life's ups and downs. These are the people who stick with you through job losses, bankruptcies, divorces, and those days when life feels overwhelming. They love you when you feel like you have nothing to give.

I have maybe a dozen casual friends whom I adore, and three really close friendships that go much deeper. That's not to say that every friend in your life has to be a lifer. Friends aren't all meant to play the same role. What causes unnecessary heartache is when we expect one friend to show up like another. That's what I call Friendship Theater—when we cast people in roles they were never meant to play.

One of my dear friends, Betsy, is my "fun friend," the ultimate party girl. She throws the best events and surrounds herself with a constant swirl of fun, energy, and excitement. But to Betsy, *I'm* not necessarily the "fun friend." I don't get invited to every brunch or birthday bash, and I'm totally OK with that. To her, and most of my close friends for that matter, I'm the "friend you call when you need help."

Betsy was in a serious four-wheeler accident, and I was one of only two friends she called to sit by her bedside at the hospital. When another friend was diagnosed with brain cancer, she called me to go with her to surgery in Phoenix. When my friends or their children need help finding a job, I'm the one they call. I've embraced my role as the "resource" friend, and I love that I can show up for my people in this way.

You've got friends you dream with, friends you vacation with, and friends you can have fun with even if you're just running errands. There's no "best" type of friend, but understanding the role I play in my friends' lives and the role they play in mine has freed me from unnecessary pain.

Instead of asking, "Why didn't I get invited to that dinner?" I can look through the photos, smile, and think, "Of course I wasn't invited to this. That's not who I am to her!" Instead of wondering why a friend didn't show up for me during a hard time, I can find peace knowing that's simply not her purpose in my life.

I wish someone had explained this to me back when friendship dynamics made me feel jealous, resentful, or left out. Figure out the real purpose people are meant to serve in your life— don't cast them in a role they can't fulfill. When you stop confusing seasonal friends with ride-or-die friends, you're free to prioritize the relationships that bring the most meaning to your world.

How Do You Find Ride-or-Die Friends?

My one piece of advice to all women is to find your people, love them hard, and invest in them. They will be there for support when you need each other. But how do you know who your people are? It helps to have a clear idea of what a ride-or-die friendship looks like to you. For me, it boils down to three things: time, distance, and silence

Time is important because life gets busy. It's an unrealistic expectation that you and your friends will be able to catch up weekly or monthly in some seasons. There may be long periods when you don't see each other or communicate much, but this person isn't going anywhere, no matter how much time passes.

Distance matters because life can take our closest people far away. Distance can be geographical or simply life pulling you in different directions. You could be chasing different dreams or living hundreds of miles apart, but you still stop to check in and cheer each other on.

Silence is challenging because life can get heavy. We disappear into our own mess for a while and real friends don't take that personally. It's a bond you both trust enough to pick back up when you're ready.

If a friendship can survive all three—time, distance, and silence—you know you've got a real one on your hands.

Real friends respect each other's journeys, even when life paths diverge. It's not about always being on the same page, but about wanting the best for each other and genuinely celebrating each other's wins.

I love this saying: "You lie to your friends, and I'll lie to mine, but let's not lie to each other." To me, that's the core of real friendship: truth without pretense. "Being real" means showing up as your true self, warts and all, and giving the people in your life permission to do the same. Letting people see the real you is how you get deep enough to find those lifelong friendships.

For a long time, I thought I wasn't lonely because I was always surrounded by people. Coworkers, meetings, team retreats, work events, and client calls. But when no one knows the real you, it doesn't matter how many people are in your life. You'll eventually crave *real* friends and true connection.

Don't Wait Until You're Lonely

In my 30s, I let my friendships slip. I felt so guilty about working all the time that I only allowed myself to be a mom or a worker. If I wasn't working, I was being a mom. I didn't invest in friendships because that took more time away from my kids.

Maybe you've had the thought I repeated to myself during that time: "I'm just in a busy season." But seasons turn into decades if you're not careful. I put my head down and barreled ahead in my career for years without investing much in my social circle. I woke up one day when I was around 45 years old and thought, "Oh no! Where are all my friends?"

At work, I was surrounded by smart, funny, capable women, but they lived all across the globe. We couldn't see each other on weekends. I couldn't show up on their birthdays to hand-deliver their favorite coffee. We couldn't take one look at each other and know something was off without needing to ask. We didn't know each other like that.

If you're balancing work and family, don't abandon your friendships. Don't wake up in your mid-40s wishing you'd scheduled check-ins with people you've long since lost touch with.

Even if you barely have time or energy to spare, know that friendship isn't a luxury. It's an essential part of life. It doesn't take big nights out or fancy girls' trips to keep them going. Sometimes, a small gesture can be the shot in the arm that keeps a friendship alive. Here are a few ideas to help you show a friend you care this week:

- Send a quick voice note instead of typing out a long text.
- Drop off a coffee or have it delivered during a friend's lunch break
- Invite someone for a walk instead of waiting for a perfect dinner date.
- Schedule a ten-minute window on your calendar once a week to check in with someone you haven't spoken to in a while.

Life's a trip, so if you're hanging on by a thread, I guarantee your friends feel it too. Don't wait for the perfect moment to let them know you're right there with them. Don't tell yourself you'll reach out when work slows down or when the kids need you less. Remind yourself that a tiny gesture is good enough.

The connections you nurture today become the shoulders you lean on tomorrow. So if you wake up like I did, wondering where your friends are, it can be valuable to widen your inner circle. When I started growing my social circle again, I connected with women in completely different life stages than my own. One of the greatest surprises and blessings of my adult life has been multigenerational friendship.

Multigenerational Friendship

Like most people, I used to gravitate toward friends my age. It felt natural. We were all going through the same stuff. But now, some of the best, wisest, most life-giving women in my world are 10, 20, 30 years older than me. For years, I've been part of a group of women from all different generations. We share advice, hold space for each other, swap stories, laugh hard, and cry when we need to.

I look back now and think about the older women I met at the start of my career. Maybe if I'd been more open to friendship with them, I would've made different choices about the job that didn't fit or the marriage I wasn't ready for. Sometimes, just having someone say "I've been there" can shift everything.

On the other side of the coin, my older friends say that friendships with younger women keep them young, and you can tell. I have friends in their 60s and 70s who are every bit as exuberant as women half their age. You're not too out of touch. We all have gifts to give and receive from one another. The most unexpected pairings have the most to offer us if we're open to that possibility.

It doesn't have to be hard to expand your circle. Reach out to someone from work, a church group, or even your partner's family and ask: "I'd love to learn from you. Can we grab a cup of coffee?"

Life is richer when you have a variety of perspectives in your community, rather than surrounding yourself with people who are just like you. What's more important than age or common interests is building relationships where support and respect flow both ways.

Healthy Boundaries and Mutual Care

As women, we're conditioned to nurture, give, and overextend ourselves. It's easy to slip into relationships where one person gives and gives while the other takes. If you find yourself constantly drained after interacting with a friend, step back and ask, "Am I the only one doing the giving here?"

This doesn't mean walking away from every friendship that hits a rough patch. Notice patterns and be brave enough to name them. The ability to respect each other's boundaries (both the boundaries you set and the ones your friends set for themselves) is where a friendship lives or dies.

All relationships in your life should be mutually beneficial: friends, family, and colleagues. The bonds in your life should be fulfilling, not draining. You shouldn't be the only one giving.

Ask yourself regularly:

- Is this friendship balanced?
- Are we both being nourished?
- Is there a mutual benefit here?
- Do I feel safe, seen, and respected?

If not, you're doing your friend and yourself a favor by stepping back to examine things. After all, the goal is to cultivate relationships that leave you feeling more whole, not more depleted, and to offer the same for your social circle.

Community Is a Survival Strategy

Humans have been communal beings since the dawn of time. We've survived by gathering around fires, sharing resources, and showing up for each other. And we need our

OUTSIDE OF FAMILY AND WORK, ONE OF YOUR MOST IMPORTANT RESPONSIBILITIES IS TO FIND AND NURTURE REAL FRIENDSHIPS.

people as much now as we ever have. Outside of family and work, one of your most important responsibilities is to find and nurture real friendships.

Know the roles people play in your life (the fun friend, the resource friend, the lifer, or the one who's here for a season) and honor them for who they are. The friendships that outlast life's challenges are worth prioritizing, even if all you can offer some days is a quick check in or a kind word.

Your village doesn't need to be big. You just need a few ride or dies in your corner, the women who know the real you and choose you anyway. When life falls apart, they're the ones who'll help you pick up the pieces. And that kind of love is everything.

CHAPTER 3
Romantic Relationships

The single most important decision in your life is who you choose to spend it with.

Remember Dr. Caldwell, the marriage counselor from chapter 1 who helped me see the role my family played in my relationship issues with my first husband? Here's the part where he really screwed me up.

Dr. Caldwell and I spent years unpacking my family and relationship baggage during our sessions. It felt like he knew me better than most people. That's why I took to heart what he said to me one day while discussing the possible end of my marriage. I'll never forget his words: "Robin, you've got *so* much damage and trauma that if I put you in a room with 100 men, I could point out the guys you'd be attracted to. You'll just keep choosing the same type of person, so you might as well stay married to the one you're with now."

I was shocked. Dr. Caldwell knew how unhappy I was. He knew my husband well. He knew my past. And he didn't see a better outcome for me than the situation I was in. So I thought, *well, if he really thinks that, I guess he's right. I must be doomed to always pick people who aren't nice to me. Maybe the devil I know is better than the devil I don't know.*

When Dr. Caldwell uttered those words, I took divorce off the table and didn't consider it again until years later. Three decades have passed since then, and I finally see what Dr. Caldwell was *trying* to say to me. However, here's what he *should* have said:

"We need to get you healthy. You won't always pick people who are wrong for you if you're healthy. Let's do the hard work to get you to a place where you believe you deserve to be treated well, so you can receive the kind of love that's good for you."

Back then, I wouldn't have known what kind of love was good for me. There isn't one right way to give or receive love, so how do we figure out what we need in the first place? One way I came to know these things about myself was by learning about the 5 Love Languages.

What's Your Love Language?

In his book, *The 5 Love Languages: The Secret to Love that Lasts*, Dr. Gary Chapman defines one of the best tools I've ever discovered for understanding relationships—the five distinct ways to communicate love to someone. The idea is that each of us gives and receives love best in a specific way. If your partner doesn't approach you using your love language, or you don't approach them using theirs, you're more likely to feel disconnected.

Here are the 5 Love Languages—but with my own unique take on each. The descriptions show what you can do for your partner and the examples show what they can do for you if that is *your* love language.

1. **Direct Positive Encouragement.** You need spoken words of appreciation. Talk isn't cheap—and words are free—so let them flow.
   Example: Your partner says, "I know how hard you worked on that project. Your dedication blows me away."

2. **Find a Need, Fill a Need.** You do what needs to be done for your partner—without them having to ask.
   Example: They notice your gas tank is low and fill it up before you head to work.

3. **A Trinket for Your Thoughts.** Notice what they like and give it to them to show they are valued.
   Example: They bring home chocolate ice cream after a long day because they remembered you mentioned it.

4. **The Gift of Your Presence.** Put down your phone and invest in the other person with your full attention.
   Example: They invite you on a walk to catch up and hear what's on your heart.

5. **The Sweet Spot.** It's like the intersection of a Venn diagram—but with your physical bodies. This happens when your molecules mingle: holding hands or sitting closet together on the couch.
   Example: They pull you in for a hug when you're overwhelmed.

In a healthy relationship, you can use the love languages to get closer to your partner or learn what friends, family members, or colleagues need from you. For example, I could tell my husband, "I feel closest to you when you tell me what I mean to you." Or he could tell me, "What I really want tonight is for us to eat dinner without our phones."

In unhealthy relationships, asking for what you need can lead to more conflict. Your needs may be ignored, dismissed, or used against you.

When Needs Become Weapons

Understanding the 5 Love Languages helped me put words to what I'd always needed in a relationship. But it also helped me see something more painful: When someone who wants to hurt you knows your love language, they can use it as a weapon.

> **WHEN SOMEONE WHO WANTS TO HURT YOU KNOWS YOUR LOVE LANGUAGE, THEY CAN USE IT AS A WEAPON.**

My first husband and I once hosted a wedding shower at our house. A few of the husbands were hitting golf balls into the yard, and I decided to join them. One of them complimented me, "Wow, Robin, you have a great golf swing!"

My ex cut in immediately. "Oh, you have no idea. She's got a good swing, but she can't hit the ball." Then, he started throwing balls down in front of me to prove his point. "Go on, show them. Try to hit that one."

Every now and then I'd hit a good shot, but I also hit several shanks. Eventually, I threw my club down and said, "Well, I'm done with this!"

My ex laughed, "See, I told y'all she can't hit the ball."

Later that night, I asked if anyone wanted to get in the pool. Everyone said yes, but the women hadn't brought their swimsuits. My ex-husband said, "Robin has been every size in the book. Let me go get hers." He came back with a wad of my swimsuits from every stage of my life and proceeded to show them all, one by one, to the whole room full of people.

"Here," he said, "this one's from when she weighed 200 pounds."

He held up one of my maternity swimsuits, and the room fell silent. The women glanced at each other and me, totally mortified. Our friends made polite conversation about how it was getting late, and they decided to head home instead of going for a swim.

Although we didn't know the vocabulary around love languages back then, my first husband knew kind words meant a lot to me, and he used that knowledge against me. Instead of words of affirmation, I got words of humiliation.

If your deepest needs are consistently turned against you, that's a gigantic red flag, even if it's the only way you've seen a relationship work. Reflecting on that story reminded me that I'd seen something similar play out for another woman in my life: my mother.

The Flying Christmas Tree

What I went through wasn't unique in my family. I'd seen a similar pain show up in my mom's life as well. When I was a child, my mom packed her car full of knickknacks to sell at a neighbor's garage sale, including a few small gifts my stepdad had given her over the years. She wanted to clear the house of items we weren't using anymore to bring in some extra money for Christmas. Somehow, my stepdad found out, and he repurchased every item that he'd given my mom. He wrapped them up and shoved them under our Christmas tree.

My mom's love language is receiving gifts. So when we came downstairs on Christmas morning, she was excited to open all the presents under the tree, addressed with love from her husband.

One by one, she opened each item she'd sold at the garage sale. At first, she looked confused and then hurt when she realized what was happening. Meanwhile, the smug look on my stepdad's face made it clear that this wasn't some misguided attempt at sentimentality. His eyes lit up with rage, and I saw that he was punishing my mother. Our happy Christmas morning shifted when my stepdad smashed glass decorations into the floor while berating my mom. How dare she sell gifts he probably hadn't thought about in years?

He worked himself into a frenzy, and finally, I watched in horror as he hurled the entire Christmas tree, complete with tinsel and my hand-painted ornaments, straight through the living room. Pine needles and shattered ornaments fell meeting the piles of shredded wrapping paper covering the living room floor.

Weaponizing the most meaningful thing to my mom—gifts— was the deepest cut my stepdad could make and on some level, he knew that. Just like my first husband knew using words against me would hurt more than anything.

These experiences reinforced a dark belief in my mind. It wasn't just unrealistic to have my needs met in healthy ways; it wasn't something I deserved.

Consequences of Unhealed Wounds and Unmet Needs

All living things suppress our needs temporarily to stay safe. Animals stop eating when predators are near because the most pressing need is staying alive. Eventually though, they need to eat again. Our needs must be met, so we can't live forever in survival mode. But try explaining that to a woman who spent her childhood in survival mode. Why should she suddenly get her needs met now?

Toward the end of my first marriage, I was depleted but hanging on because all signs pointed to life not getting any better from here. We weren't giving or receiving what we needed from each other, no matter how much counseling we did. My mind said, *This is just how it goes.* My heart, on the other hand, was still quietly fighting to meet my needs, even if it meant abandoning my values.

That's how I found myself tangled in an emotional affair with a coworker. We'll call him Luke. He told me I was smart, sought my opinions, and valued what I had to say. It was nothing physical at first. He gave me the words of affirmation I had been starved for.

Eventually, I couldn't go a day without talking to him. I was beaten down emotionally and mentally at home. This relationship made me feel seen and appreciated for the first time in years.

When things finally turned physical on a business trip, I couldn't handle the guilt. I confessed to my husband and begged for forgiveness. The crazy part was that Luke and I were only physical the one time. I didn't care about that; it was the emotional aspect that felt so hard to let go.

But I knew it had to end. I cut things off with Luke that same week. My husband was understandably furious, but he said he wanted to try to work through it. We went back to counseling and tried to patch things up. But our relationship was already so broken; this was the last nail in the coffin.

Shaming myself was my first instinct. But what I really needed was to understand how I had ended up there in the first place. Unhealed wounds don't

> **UNHEALED WOUNDS DON'T JUSTIFY BAD CHOICES, BUT THEY CAN HELP EXPLAIN THEM.**

justify bad choices, but they can help explain them. And when those wounds go unattended, they can lead us to abandon our needs altogether.

The thing is, you can't ignore the pain in your heart forever and expect to be the only one affected by your self-abandonment. This is why healing is so much more than an act of self-care.

Healing is your responsibility to the people you love.

I didn't know what I needed to heal at the time; I just knew I couldn't keep going like this. I called a friend and said, "I need to get away." In my desperation, I was grasping for answers, or at least a place where the noise would stop. A few days later,

I found myself driving to her family's cabin in the middle of nowhere with a stack of self-help books and journals.

Nervous Breakdown at the Cabin

When I opened that cabin door and dropped my bags, I didn't feel relieved. I felt like I didn't want my life anymore. I didn't want to be in this world anymore. I crawled into bed and stared at the ceiling, still fully dressed, tears rolling into my hairline.

No kids.

No husband.

No calls.

But there it was—the pain I could no longer outrun.

The next morning, I forced myself out of bed, brewed some coffee, and picked up a workbook by Dr. Phil. I thought maybe it would help me make sense of the relationship baggage that led me here. I flipped to a section that suggested writing out significant moments in your life.

"What's your first memory?" the book prompted.

My first memory is when my parents told me they were getting divorced. I was 7 years old.

"Describe how the memory played out."

After they told me, I put on a baseball cap, jumped on my bicycle, and rode around the neighborhood to process the sadness. I was repeating that pattern here, running away from my heartache of a relationship's end.

I continued the exercises until one question stopped me in my tracks.

"What lie do you believe about yourself?"

There was something about that question that opened the floodgates for me. I dropped the book, curled into the fetal position, and started rocking back and forth like a baby.

The lie I'd spent my life believing came to me so clearly at that moment: **If my own mother didn't love me enough to protect me from my abusive stepdad, then I must be unlovable.**

I realized that nearly every decision I'd made in relationships up to that point was connected to this toxic belief. I married someone who was wrong for me. I constantly tried to keep the peace and make others happy. I didn't consider what my needs were because I didn't think they deserved to be met. All of it came from the belief my mother never intended to instill in me—that I was unlovable.

As much as I hate to admit it, sometimes hitting rock bottom really is the best catalyst for change. It didn't happen overnight. But after my nervous breakdown at the cabin, I started taking steps toward a better relationship with myself. That meant I could no longer ignore that my marriage needed to end. My first husband and I finally divorced in 2004 after nine years with one son and one daughter.

When I was ready to date again, I told myself I didn't want anyone who was anything like my stepdad or my first husband. I wanted the total opposite. So that's what I did: I swung hard in the other direction.

Overcorrecting and Getting It Wrong

My stepdad was an alcoholic who had angry, violent outbursts, and my first husband was just plain mean. So when I met my second husband, a man who was totally passive and conflict-avoidant, I thought, *This must be what safety looks like.*

I married him way too quickly. That wasn't fair to either of us. I had identified my unhealthy relationship patterns, but I hadn't healed from them yet. I was still letting my trauma steer me, just down a different road.

We had two sons together, and I wouldn't trade being their mom for anything in the world. But looking back on my first two marriages from a place of healing, I can say

> **I WAS THE COMMON DENOMINATOR IN MY SUFFERING, NOT MY FIRST OR SECOND HUSBAND.**

something I never would've admitted before. Despite Dr. Caldwell's awful delivery, he was right in a way. It didn't really matter who I married during that season of my life. It was going to be a dumpster fire. I was the common denominator in my suffering, not my first or second husband.

Were there things they could have done better? Absolutely. They weren't perfect, but I wasn't either. My emotional, mental, and spiritual health was in such a bad place that I was incapable

> **I KNEW HOW TO BE BUSY, HOW TO ACHIEVE, AND HOW TO SURVIVE. BUT WHEN IT CAME TO CREATING A STRONG, INTIMATE PARTNERSHIP, I WAS CLUELESS.**

of giving or receiving healthy love from anyone, including myself. That's the absolute rock-bottom truth.

I wasn't curious about what I needed. I wasn't intentional with how I communicated or connected. I was reacting to my past more than making conscious, grounded choices in my own best interest. I knew how to be busy, how to achieve, and how to survive. But when it came to creating a strong, intimate partnership, I was clueless.

Do I Even Know How to Be a Wife?

After I married Shannon, my third and forever husband, my dad gave me a compliment I didn't fully understand. He said, "It's nice to see you being a girl, Robin." I shrugged it off at first. But later, I understood what he meant.

I'd been a strong woman my whole life. I knew how to hustle, provide, raise babies, lead teams, and manage a household. But I didn't know how to let myself be taken care of. I didn't know how to be soft and truly relax in a relationship.

And honestly, I didn't know how to be a good wife. I hadn't made it a priority. I used to think being a good wife was about cooking, doing laundry, buying groceries, having sex, and keeping the house running. As I began my third marriage, I didn't stop to ask what kind of partner I wanted to be for the man I'd chosen to spend my life with. I didn't think about the deeper traits he needed in our relationship, like mutual respect, loyalty, good communication, acceptance, support, and encouragement.

I can say with confidence that I was not a good wife to my first two husbands. Good wife traits still don't come naturally to me. The women in my family did a great job taking care of the house and the kids, but I didn't see them prioritize their husbands.

Marrying Shannon was the first time that I *wanted* to be a good wife, but I wasn't sure how to get there. This man is my soulmate, and yet I almost ran him off too.

Real Love Takes Real Trust

I guess I'm like Goldilocks. My first marriage was too hard. My second was too soft. But my marriage with Shannon is just right. That doesn't mean it's perfect. It means we have our issues, we know how to work them out, and we'll gladly spend the rest of our lives doing that.

Shannon and I met when I was in 7th grade, and he was a senior in high school. He broke up with his cheerleader girlfriend and asked my mom if he could date me. Of course, she said no. We became good friends but eventually, life pulled us in different directions.

We hadn't spoken in decades when we reconnected at a high school reunion in Arkansas. One conversation turned into eight hours. We tried to warn each other: I was a single mom with four kids and two ex-husbands, and he was separated but couldn't get his ex to sign divorce papers.

But there was no use fighting it. It was like we picked up where we'd left off in 1985, except now the timing was right. We talked every day after that reunion, and we've been together ever since.

But even with a foundation like that, trust still gets tested.

Soon after we started dating, Shannon called to tell me that he was headed on a vacation with his kids and soon-to-be ex-wife. He promised he'd stay in a separate room away from the rest of the family. But I was furious.

We'd made a deal that we'd never lie to one another, and this felt like a decision he made without considering me. That's when Shannon said something I'll never forget: "Robin, every decision I make is with your best interest in mind. You might not like this decision. You might not see why I'm doing it, but the intent behind every decision I make is to take care of you. To take care of us."

Shannon explained that by going on this trip, he thought he could finally get his separated wife to sign the divorce papers she'd been dodging—so the two of us could get married.

He went on, "If you can't trust me when I don't do what you want me to do, that's not trust at all. So you need to take this time to decide whether you can trust me."

He went on the trip while I stayed home alone, crying in the fetal position. Suddenly, I was 32 again in that cabin in the woods, breaking down over a relationship that might be doomed. But this time, it was a relationship that felt right in every way.

I asked myself, *Robin, can you trust someone who doesn't do what you want them to do? Can you trust Shannon Goad with your heart? With your life?*

I realized that even healthy love takes deep, inner work that can feel like it's ripping you apart. But you know what else feels like that? Growth. I wasn't falling apart in isolation this time. I wasn't reeling after I was brought to a breaking point from destructive behavior. I was fighting for the love of my life. This was a healthy love that I'd found my way back to after years of hard-as-hell healing work.

That's the kind of love I never thought I'd have—the kind worth fighting for. It's the kind of love I want every woman to know is still possible, no matter what she's been through.

I battled with myself all weekend long, but finally I decided, *If I can't trust Shannon then who can I trust?* I made the right decision. We were married on November 11, 2011 (11-11-11).

You're a Cycle-Breaker Too

No matter your age, your battle scars, or the number of times you've gotten it wrong, know that it's never too late to have your "happily ever after." It's not easy, and it sure won't look like a fairytale most of the time. But nothing is more worthwhile than the kind of love built on healing, honesty, and the daily decision to keep battling it out side by side.

With the right love, you won't have to fight to feel worthy. You'll feel safe enough to fall apart, knowing your partner and the connection you share are strong enough to hold you as you rebuild.

The work it takes to get healthy, trust again, and love *yourself* enough to receive the love that meets your needs is life-changing. But it's not just for you. Building healthy relationships is an act of preventive care for your kids, your community, and anyone else watching your life up close.

If I hadn't uncovered the old lie that I was unlovable and worked to heal it, I wondered: *Would my kids carry the same story into their relationships? Would they make destructive choices like the ones I made?* If healing means I take the hit so my kids don't have to, I'll do that every time.

You don't have to keep passing down lies that were never meant to shape your life. Let that cycle stop with you.

I don't know about you, but the legacy I want stamped on my family tree isn't: "She suppressed her needs to keep everyone happy."

It's: "She got healthy, and we all learned what real love can look like."

CHAPTER 4

Parenting

Don't judge yourself or your kids until they're at least 30!

Parenting is about raising emotionally, physically, and spiritually healthy children. But let's say the quiet part out loud: It's also the most shame-ridden job on the planet.

From the moment that baby arrives, you're making decisions that can lead to shame someday, if not immediately. Vaccines or no vaccines? Breast milk or formula? Timeouts or spankings? Daycare or nanny? You can do hours of research, talk to every wise woman you know, pray about it, and still look back later and realize you got it wrong.

The truth is, raising a child is the greatest experiment in human history. You mix two people's DNA with outside opinions, stress, sleepless nights, and maybe some childhood baggage you haven't dealt with yet, toss it all in a blender with zero instructions, and expect to make no mistakes. It simply ain't gonna happen.

Mistakes are inevitable, and that's where the shame and guilt start to creep in.

The pressure and focus on "getting it right" for the kids means we often forget to take care of ourselves. I honestly believe I was the worst version of myself in the early days of mothering. I wish I had paused and thought about what would matter most when I'm in my 80s and when my kids are in their 80s.

When I look back, I won't wish I'd kept the house tidier or packed the most balanced lunches. I'll ask myself, *Did I set them up to have healthy relationships, marriages, and friendships? Did I give them the tools to find careers they love or faith that sticks?* The way we parent plays a role in all of this.

I had my first two children, Macy and Carter, with my first husband, and my second two children, Graham and Spencer, years later with my second husband. I'd be lying if I said I parented them all the same. I wasn't the same woman, and I didn't have the same wisdom for the first two as I did for the second two.

When I became a mom, I thought the job description was to make (and keep) my kids happy. That's what I saw growing up. My mother tried to keep me happy by buying me things and never telling me "no." Maybe that was her way of overcompensating for the emotional mess we often lived in. I inherited that mindset without realizing it, and when Macy and Carter came along, I ran with it.

I bent over backward with the goal of keeping them content. If they were sad or disappointed, I took it personally. If they asked for something, I found a way to give it even if it cost me sleep, money, or sanity.

But over time, I started to see flaws in that approach. I wasn't leading; I was people-pleasing my way through motherhood. That wore me out and did my kids a disservice. By trying to fix their problems and shield them from discomfort, I robbed them of chances to navigate conflict and build resilience.

While raising my younger two sons, Graham and Spencer, I've had a different perspective. As I became the healthier, more mature person I wanted to be, I could be a much better mom for them. I realized that children need love, but they also need boundaries. They need to know someone is steering the ship. If you let them dictate how you parent, it will always be about what they want right now, not what's best for them down the road.

The truth is, getting to raise children in two very different seasons of life gave me a rare gift: a chance to course-correct. By the time I had my younger two, I'd seen how my early choices had played out with my oldest two. I could hold firm on the things I knew mattered and let go of the patterns that hadn't served any of us.

Before you become a mother, it's impossible to understand how much parenting will stretch you and how many of your unhealed places it will uncover. We see so many highlight reels of motherhood, but I think we'd benefit from more real-life, imperfect motherhood stories. We need more honest perspectives on the tough stuff we often navigate alone.

I hope my unique motherhood journey, raising two sets of kids with two exes and my husband Shannon, can give you real perspectives. Whether you're a new mom just figuring it out, a grandmother watching your own children raise theirs, or someone who never had kids but carries the emotional load of caregiving, motherhood leaves a lasting impact on us all. How our mothers treated us. The expectations society puts on us to become mothers and do it *this* way. The many possible ways to get it wrong.

I want to pass along some of the wisdom and experiences I gained the hard way. And I wish I could share them with my younger self so she'd feel less alone. One of the biggest shifts I made with my younger two children was learning to parent with the future in mind, not the emotions in front of me.

Parenting with the Future in Mind

If I could go back and speak to 30-year-old Robin who was newly navigating motherhood, the one who believed she was responsible for keeping her children happy, here's what I'd say to her: Guaranteeing your child's happiness might *feel* like your job as a mother, but it isn't. Trying to make that the job will drain you and hinder them in the process.

Think about the future. Think about the adult they'll grow up to be.

Your job is to be strong enough to let them struggle sometimes. Let them experience disappointment. Let them fail and learn they can brush themselves off and get back up again.

Kids who only experience ease, joy, and the word "yes" won't be able to handle "no." They expect the world to bend for them and when it doesn't, they don't know how to bounce back. My oldest son, Carter, had the hardest time with authority, and it wasn't because he was a bad kid. It was because I didn't establish firm boundaries early on.

When Carter was two, I became a single mom. Through the years, without meaning to, I made him my co-parent. Carter fixed the TV and helped me with things as a little "man of the house." His first-grade teacher told me it was like having an adult in the room because he got all of her jokes. At the time, I was proud. I thought I was raising a wise and capable boy. But really, I was placing the weight of an adult role on his little shoulders.

I gave my older kids a seat at the adult table before they were ready. I wanted to be honest, and I didn't want to hide the hard stuff. But in doing that, I caused them to see me as an equal rather than an adult to trust and respect.

When my husband, Shannon, came into the picture nine years later, Macy was 14, Carter was 11, Graham was 5, and Spencer was 4. Shannon was shocked by our family dynamic. He said, "Robin, you're killing yourself. You're juggling four children, two ex-husbands, and your mother. And nobody is taking care of you." His approach rubbed against my parenting style up to that point, but I knew he was right.

Shannon wasn't afraid to challenge Carter and tell him "no." Because of how I raised him, Carter didn't like that one bit. Carter and Shannon went head-to-head, and their clash was hard to accept. I almost ended our marriage over this conflict. But it forced me to face the fact that I'd handed over too much power too early. It helped me see the path I'd rather choose with my younger ones.

I don't think I parented the way I did in the beginning because I wanted to be my kids' best friend. I wanted *easy*. I wanted *peace*. I wanted everyone to be happy, even if that meant giving them everything they wanted. I didn't want to be their favorite over their dads, but I did want them to like me. I wanted them to see that I was always willing to do whatever it took to make them happy.

That's why I say now: Don't let yourself believe that making them happy or being liked by your children should be the highest goal. In fact, if you want to like them when they're adults, get comfortable with not being their favorite person while they're young. That closeness comes later if you've earned their respect by being their anchor first.

Your kids may not always like your rules, but they'll trust them. They'll know your boundaries are strong enough to lean on. That's how you become their rock. Be the parent who's willing to make the hard decisions now, and eventually, they'll see that everything you did was from a place of love.

Parenting can't be about your kids' happiness today because you're not taking care of a toddler who has a meltdown over a snack. You're raising someone who will one day have to navigate a breakup, handle a work conflict, and maybe raise kids of their own. How they manage emotions, respond to authority, and care for others starts in their childhood.

Boundaries and Consequences

Here's the unfortunate truth that Shannon helped me see: If you don't set boundaries when they're young, you'll face much harder consequences later.

The adorable little boy who thinks you hung the moon might grow up to be a middle schooler who says cruel things or won't even speak to you. If you don't teach your kids to follow the rules when they're three, they won't think the rules of the road apply to them when you buy them a car at 16.

Respecting authority gets more important as they get older and the consequences of not doing so get more serious. The kid who gets her way by kicking and screaming on the floor of the toy store becomes the teenager who gets caught driving under the influence because she didn't think there'd be any consequences.

The consequences of raising children this way ripple out to other family members too. I grew up in a family that revolved around children and placed them at the top of the hierarchy. The children in our family mattered more than the men. So when my mom saw that Shannon was shifting the dynamic in my household, she didn't like it. She told me it'd drive a wedge between my kids and me. At one point, she even wanted me to leave him over this topic.

Luckily, I had one good friend who spoke the truth. Stephanie had the courage, conviction, and love to sit me down and tell me that I was the problem, not Shannon. She helped me see that Shannon was trying to set some order. His intention was to establish healthy boundaries and a clear hierarchy in this family.

Thank God for Stephanie. If she hadn't spoken that truth to me, I might have divorced my wonderful husband. (Sidenote here girls: Make sure you have a friend who will say the hard things you need to hear. Not what you *want* to hear but *need* to hear.)

And I get it. When you've seen it as your duty to make your kids happy, structure feels like punishment. But I had to decide: Was I going to parent based on guilt and obligation or based on what I knew would help them become responsible, healthy adults?

Here's something I've learned the hard way: There are three primary sources of conflict in most marriages, especially once kids come into the picture.

1. Parenting issues
2. Money issues
3. Family issues (his and yours)

It starts as arguments over daycare versus hiring a nanny or formula versus breast milk. Mom and dad conflicts are absolutely inevitable. But your partnership is the foundation of the entire family. You were a family before you ever had children and you'll be a family after the kids have left to start their own families. The boundaries you set now aren't only to help your children thrive in adulthood. They help your relationship survive their childhood too.

Even today, when one of my kids asks me to do something, my first instinct is still, "Of course. What can I do?" But that's the old muscle memory talking. That's performance-based love, rather than me checking in with my boundaries.

One of the best ways to shift that pattern is to pause and ask: *Is this something I truly want to do? Or am I saying yes out of guilt or obligation?*

Learning to set healthy boundaries is hard enough when you have a solid marriage, but what about parenting through other dynamics? As a mom co-parenting with two exes and my husband, I'd like to tell you what I wish I'd known about going through divorce as a mother.

Parenting Through Divorce

If you're a mom navigating or thinking about divorce, here are some things I wish someone had sat me down and ensured I truly understood. Divorce means you only get half the summer holidays, half the Christmas holidays, and half the weekends. Fifty percent of your kids' time is spent away from you, which gives you less time to be their mom during the years that already fly by.

The issues you have with their dad don't go away. In many cases, they get more complicated. Once you have children with someone, their presence in your life doesn't disappear. It just shifts. You're now parenting across separate households with separate values and routines. You're still navigating school forms, discipline, pickups, and hard conversations together, even if the relationship is strained.

Here's something I wish every divorced mom could hear: Don't speak badly about your kids' dad. No matter how small you think the comment is, it matters. Your kids are half you and half him. When you say something negative about their dad, they feel like you're saying it about them. Divorce doesn't mean you can stop biting your tongue if you have less-than-positive opinions about your ex. You still have to be intentional with your words for your children's sake.

I don't say any of this to dissuade you. You have to find the right answer for your situation. Divorce was still the right answer for me in the end. But I do wish I'd thought more about the time I was giving up with my kids and the fact that their dads would still be intertwined in my life.

Divorce was one of the factors that led me to parent out of guilt. Another was a phase of my life that happened long before my children were born.

What's Your "Parenting Lens?"

When I was young, I made a series of decisions that changed my identity as a mother before I ever became one—I had three abortions. We'll talk more about my abortion journey in chapter 8, but I wanted to name it here because sometimes the guilt we carry as mothers doesn't start with our kids. It started much further back in our past.

In my postabortion healing work, I learned that many women who have abortions in their past, myself included, carry this feeling in their hearts even if they don't realize it. Once my children were born, there was a thought buried deep inside me: *Why did I keep these four babies, and not my other three?*

That guilt shaped how I parented, especially in the early years. It also caused me to have a harder time connecting with my children. I didn't feel that automatic protectiveness that I'd assumed came naturally to every mom. I thought there must be something wrong with me. I'd say things like, "Man, maybe I just don't have the nurturing gene."

Now I see what was really happening. I'd numbed the "nurturing" feeling subconsciously to protect myself from unprocessed pain. It was like my brain turned off my desire to protect my children because if I felt that for them, that'd mean I'd have to feel it for the babies I aborted too. I'd have to reckon with all the trauma I'd buried.

When you're trying to survive, you can't be who you really are because you're in a constant state of fight or flight. If we aren't operating from a place of strength, stability, and security for ourselves, how in the world can we provide it for the kids?

> IF WE AREN'T OPERATING FROM A PLACE OF STRENGTH, STABILITY, AND SECURITY FOR OURSELVES, HOW IN THE WORLD CAN WE PROVIDE IT FOR THE KIDS?

Parenting from an unhealed place means everything gets filtered through a warped lens. In some ways, that guilt made me over-give and people-please my children. But in other ways, it hardened me. I took on this belief that the world was a tough place, so I needed to toughen my kids up before it got to them first. That mindset showed up in my tone, my discipline, and how quickly I dismissed their emotions.

That lens of numbed-out trauma meant I couldn't see beyond the day in front of us a lot of the time. I wish I'd created a space where they always felt heard and supported, but some days, we barely survived, much less thrived.

In my unhealed state, I couldn't think about how my actions today would affect my children's ability to form healthy relationships, marriages, and friendships. My compulsion to overwork might impact how their careers play out. And how the way I lived out my faith could make the difference between them knowing God or not.

Before I could play a positive role in my children's development, I had to make sure they felt emotionally secure. That sense of safety had to come from me, and the lens I operated from as a parent. If I wanted my kids to be resourceful and emotionally resilient, I needed to get healthy so my parenting aligned better with those outcomes.

A strategy that works for one kid won't work for the next. Every child is different. That's how your parenting strategy differs from your parenting lens. Adapt the strategy for each child, but the overall parenting lens shouldn't change.

Shannon was more of a disciplinarian to Graham and Spencer; my ex told him that he wasn't allowed to discipline Macy and Carter. That was a huge mistake because they would throw that back in our faces whenever a conflict came up. Shannon's approach to discipline opened my eyes to what I now see as the best parenting lens. While my firmness was a reaction to old pain, Shannon's is always through the lens of protecting the children.

It's worth asking yourself: *What lens am I parenting through? Is it guilt? Fear? Performance? People-pleasing?* Or have you done the work to clear those filters so you can parent from a place of authenticity and presence?

No matter how many mistakes you make, your kids will remember how things *felt* in their childhood. Doing the work to heal and take care of yourself gives you more clarity, allowing you to parent through a more intentional lens. That matters because long after they've forgotten the toys, the schedules, or the rules, they'll remember the emotional tone of their childhood.

Connection Over Perfection

I was a busy mom working a corporate job that involved a lot of travel. I used to think I was selfish for not making everything about my children. I didn't always have time to hand-paint a science project. Sometimes we picked up to-go food instead of having home-cooked meals. But I'll bring something like that up with my adult children and they say, "Mom, we don't remember that."

I was killing myself over things they don't remember. Go figure.

But here's something I've been surprised to find they *do* remember: "Did you show up in my world?"

This is a regret of mine. I didn't realize how much kids want you to step into their everyday lives. Come to the class parties. Go on field trips. At least every now and then.

Macy would often say, "Sheridan's mom is always at school. I wish you could be." And Carter told me once, "You never came on one field trip." I don't know if that's true or not, but that's his perception. I worked so hard every day to keep our lives running. But that's not what kids see. He just wanted me to engage in his world.

As it turns out, the things we assume are shaping our kids, like the perfectly packed lunches and fancy Christmas gifts, don't leave the biggest impact. Once they're old enough to look

AS IT TURNS OUT, THE THINGS WE ASSUME ARE SHAPING OUR KIDS, LIKE THE PERFECTLY PACKED LUNCHES AND FANCY CHRISTMAS GIFTS, DON'T LEAVE THE BIGGEST IMPACT.

back, what they remember most isn't how well you performed as a parent. It's how connected they felt to you.

If I could go back, I'd focus less on being perfect and more on being present. I'd slow *way* down. I'd make sure I didn't miss so many opportunities to ask a better question or create a meaningful conversation. When one of my kids came home and told me what little Johnny said at school, I wish I had slowed down long enough to ask, "How did that make you feel?" And then slow down enough to think, *I wonder why he feels that way.*

I missed so many good teaching moments because I was distracted, overwhelmed, or simply surviving. I wish I'd known earlier that parenting shouldn't be about survival. It should be intentional.

Intentional Parenting

Another thing you don't get out of as a parent is regret. Sorry. It's just a fact of life. But instead of sitting with those regrets, I recommend documenting the lessons. You can't turn back time. But you have more wisdom to pass to your neighbors, friends, kids, or grandkids than you might realize.

One word that always comes to my mind when I think about my parenting regrets is *intentional*. Our weeks were go-go-go. I made sure my kids and I got where we needed to be, then we came home, and we crashed in bed every night. I know survival mode is just a part of it sometimes. But if I could go back, slow down, and approach parenting with more intention, here's what I wish I'd known sooner.

1. Sometimes, all your kids need to hear is, "I get it."
2. There is no such thing as balance. You can have it all. But not at the same time.
3. No matter what you do, you'll always feel like you could have done more.
4. They're watching your behavior, not listening to what you're saying.
5. Don't shield them from the hard things.
6. Let them do their own projects! Their confidence is built by doing their own work.
7. Be real with them. Be vulnerable. I didn't realize that my kids thought I was perfect until they learned I wasn't.
8. If you have boys, let your husband make them boys. It will be uncomfortable, but if you want him to grow into a good man who respects you, I promise, it's worth it.
9. Let go of the little things! Major in the majors and let the rest go. Are you raising good people? What's their character? How's their heart? Do they have faith in themselves and others?
10. Be the loudest voice in their mind. They have so many distractions. So many voices. Fight for space in their minds and hearts.

> 11. There's no such thing as a perfect child or a perfect mom. And that's OK.
> 12. Be as flexible as possible and hold your goals loosely. Things won't always go according to plan.
> 13. It is so freaking hard. Say "I'm sorry." And say it a lot.

And finally, know that some parenting lessons will come with an extra sting. Like the time one of my sons called me out. He'd gone through a challenging time, and I talked about it with some family members. I wasn't posting his dirty laundry on social media, just confiding in people who genuinely love and care for him.

But when he found out, he simply said, "Mom, that wasn't your story to tell."

Those words hurt at the moment, but they've helped me since. I've caught myself speaking with family and thought, "Is this my story to tell?" If it's not my story, I probably shouldn't be telling it. Your children have so many helpful things to teach you. That's a gift they'll give you forever if you let them.

When It Comes Full Circle

Here's the big secret of parenthood: When you and your siblings were little, that was your parents' first time in that role. They were learning how to be parents right before your eyes. When we're kids, we don't see that. We assume the adults in our lives are all-knowing. Then you step into parenthood and realize we're all figuring it out as we go.

I can see my stepdad through that lens now. He was a deeply painful figure in my childhood, and I wouldn't wish that experience on anyone. But over the decades since, I've been able to meet the human beneath the alcoholism and aggression. While this isn't the right path for everyone, we have been able to mend our relationship.

My stepdad tried to get sober several times when I was growing up, but 22 years ago, it finally stuck. That time, he had made it far enough through The Twelve Steps of Alcoholics Anonymous that it was time to make amends with the people he'd harmed. He called me, and I forgave him. At the time, my attitude was, *You need me to forgive you? Sure, we can tick that box. But I don't want you in my life.* My first thought was to protect my kids. I didn't know that I could trust him enough to be around them.

But over the years, my stepdad slowly earned back that trust. As he redefined himself through sobriety, he kept showing up to repair our relationship. I saw evidence that he'd changed, and over time, I let him back in. He's since been to my home and attended my wedding when I married Shannon.

It took a lot of work to get here. I'm finally able to see what my mom saw back then: My stepdad is a good man with a terrible disease. He was an alcoholic who made poor choices that impacted those closest to him. But I'm grateful that my own healing allowed me to stay open so that our relationship could evolve into something redemptive and new.

The relationship between a child and parent, stepparent, or caregiver isn't always smooth sailing. I truly believe that no matter what we've been through, the human spirit in all of us *wants* to have good relationships with the people we love. It's our heart's desire to have loving connections with our parents and children. And even if we don't, we want to believe that there's potential for healing.

In my case, through behavior change and trust earned back over the years, my relationships with my stepdad *and* mom have healed from those childhood experiences. I see this as a reminder that these relationships can, and likely will, evolve over your lifetime. That's been helpful for me to hold onto because sometimes the mom you thought you'd turn out to be can feel out of reach.

Life comes at you fast, and you can't always show up how you want to as a mother. You spend years flying from guitar lessons to baseball practice to the school theater production without any time to catch your breath. Then suddenly you blink, look up at yourself in the mirror, and you're preparing to be the mother of the groom. Or you're looking at your adult daughter holding your first grandbaby, hoping your influence helps her have a good relationship with *her* kids.

There's a lot I wish I'd done differently as a mother. But recently, I found myself in another full-circle moment with my daughter during a conversation that assured me that maybe I didn't do everything wrong.

My family and I spent a hot Texas day by the pool recently, splashing around with Macy's new baby, laughing about the fire department showing up because of a false alarm. It was one of those classic summer days that feel so ordinary when you're a kid, but you realize how special they are as an adult.

Later that evening, Macy and I sat on the porch together and *really* talked for the first time since she had her son. We talked about marriage, parenting, and the hard seasons that come with each. I told her a few stories I'd never spoken aloud before—things in this book that I wanted her to hear from me first.

Toward the end of our chat, Macy looked at me and said, "Mom, I had so much fun today. I'm excited for this season of our lives. I feel like I'm finally going to get to know you as a person, not only as the mom I always thought was Superwoman. Now I get to see behind the curtain."

Mother-daughter relationships can be so charged, and ours certainly hasn't been flawless. So it touched me to hear this from her. It touched me to share such an honest moment as two women talking.

"You know," I said back. "I'm really excited about the possibility of us being friends."

She said, "Yeah. That kind of blows my mind."

We laughed and hugged before she packed up the little one to head home for the night.

I always thought I was the mom who threw good birthday parties and showed up for the big events. I didn't think I was a great mom. I thought I'd spent too much time surviving, not enough time being intentional. But if I raised a daughter

I'd want to be friends with as an adult, and who'd want to be friends with me, maybe I did something right after all.

Motherhood isn't about getting everything perfect. But if you keep showing up, love them fiercely, apologize often, and tell the truth about who you are, there's a good chance that one day, your relationship with your kids will come full circle.

You'll look at them not just with pride, but with awe. Somewhere in all the mess, all the worry, all the wondering if you were doing it right, you managed to raise a pretty cool person—someone you'd actually want to hang out with and who still wants *you* around too. There's no greater reward than that.

PART 1 REFLECTION: TIME TO GET REAL

Before you move on, take a moment and reflect on this part of your life. The questions below are here to help you get honest with yourself. You can journal your answers, talk them out with a friend, or simply sit with them for a bit. Don't be afraid to go deeper than you usually would. Slowing down long enough to really look at your life can help you understand yourself better, make meaningful changes, and become the woman you're meant to be.

1. Do you recognize any old family patterns that are holding you back today? What would it look like to loosen their grip on your life now?
2. Have you noticed red flags in any of your relationships? Can you find ways to communicate your concerns? Is it worth considering letting go?
3. Are there friends you've grown distant from and you'd like to reconnect with? Why not reach out with a quick "thinking of you" message today?
4. What do you want your kids to remember most about how you showed up for them? What about your family and friends? How can you be that person for them today?

PART 2

Your Career

Your second most important decision,
and the hardest to get right.

Second only to your relationships, your career has the greatest impact on your daily life. It's where you spend most of your waking hours. The career path you choose impacts how you feel when you get up in the morning, how much time and energy you have for the people you love, and whether you come home feeling fulfilled or just exhausted.

Your career also has a sneaky way of tying itself to your worth. People don't just ask, "What do you do?" They make assumptions about who you are based on the answer. Over time, it's easy to start believing that what you do *is* who you are.

Part 2 goes beyond work to discuss your core identity, ambition, survival, and the stories we tell ourselves about what it means to succeed. We'll explore what you *thought* you'd do with your life, what you *actually* did, and what you want now. It might not be what you thought when you started. Heck, you might want something totally different now than you did last year.

There's no better way to figure out what's next than to get real about your values, your needs, and what really lights your fire. Because it's never too late to correct course, redefine success, or uncover the work you're meant to do in this season of life.

If your career path takes you into the corporate world, here's something I've learned: It's a game. There are unspoken rules, and working hard isn't enough to win.

After more than 30 years building a remarkable career in corporate America, my next chapter is helping young professional women make a corporate success plan. I want you to avoid mistakes I made, rise through the ranks faster, and approach your career with a winning strategy.

If this sounds like the support you're looking for, visit therealrobingoad.com to reach out. I'd love to connect and explore how I can help.

CHAPTER 5

What You Thought You'd Do

You're asked to choose a career before you know who you are. Of course you didn't nail it the first time.

Before you're 20 years old, you're expected to pick a path. College or trade school? Go straight to work or start a business? How about joining the military?

Society expects children (children!) to make enormous decisions before they've learned how to do their laundry without turning everything pink, let alone figure out who they are. I want to acknowledge how crazy it is that we've put that unrealistic expectation on our young people.

I look back now and think: *How could we ever expect to get it right on the first try?*

It doesn't matter if you're in your 20s, 40s, or 60s, if you find yourself in a career that doesn't feel right, or maybe never did, this chapter is your permission slip to pause, look up, and ask: Does the path I'm on still make sense for the woman I've become?

Sometimes, what we thought we'd do wasn't really about us in the first place. It was about pleasing someone, proving something, or chasing a version of success we were sold. You could have been boxed in by one or two permissible paths mandated by your parents, or you could have been paralyzed by the sea of possibilities. Either way, the start of your career is a daunting transition.

This chapter is about those first steps on your career path, the outside influences, the inevitable mistakes, and the core of your identity that was always there just below the surface. We'll look at the paths we start on, however misguided, and the clues our younger selves hold about our best steps from here. Whether you're working, retired, raising kids, or redefining your next chapter, it's always worth taking the time to reconnect with who you are at your core.

Who's Your Barbara Walters?

In my case, my path was decided for me by the time I was 18: I was going to college. Period. End of story. I didn't get a say in the matter; it was mandatory. My mother didn't have a degree, and she was hell-bent on me getting one. So, "thou shalt go to college."

That was fine with me because I had a plan. I was going to be Barbara Walters. That's who I wanted to be from the time I was in elementary school. As the first woman anchor of a network evening news program and cohost of The Today Show, she was a huge role model of mine. But it wasn't about fame for me. I wanted to become the next Barbara Walters because I was determined to find and expose the truth. I wanted to tell people what was really going on in the world—the good, the bad, and the ugly.

So I went to school for journalism, laser-focused on that childhood dream. But once I got there, I made the painful discovery that reporting the news wasn't really about telling the truth. It was about deadlines, ratings, sound bites, and shaping narratives. It felt more like putting on SNL (*Saturday Night Live*) sketches than it did truth-telling, and that's not what I signed up for. In the end, I graduated with my communications degree, but I bailed on filling Barbara's shoes.

Many of us make decisions thinking our career will look like something we've seen on TV, like my quest to become Barbara Walters, or the kid who pursues med school because they grew up watching *Grey's Anatomy*. Often, the vision is far from reality, but it still reveals important information about who you are.

You may not end up in the role you imagined. That doesn't mean the dream was wrong. Sometimes the job title was a placeholder for something deeper. My heart's deepest desire is still to share the truth. As it turns out,

> **YOU MAY NOT END UP IN THE ROLE YOU IMAGINED. THAT DOESN'T MEAN THE DREAM WAS WRONG.**

I didn't need to become a news anchor to make that happen. That same thread has appeared in every chapter of my life. Now here I am at 53, writing a book to help more women "get real" with ourselves, so we can uncover our personal truths.

If you've walked away from the thing you thought you'd do, don't throw out the whole dream. Who was your Barbara Walters? What did you want to be when you grew up? Long before I declared I'd be Barbara Walters, the signs were already there if I knew where to look. Sometimes our earliest instincts hold the most truth.

Childhood Clues

Further back, before college and real career ambitions, I can see clues about who I was meant to be in the silly games I played at my grandmother's house.

We played pretend all the time, but I didn't gravitate toward dolls, dress-up, or tea parties. Instead, if you can believe it, I played "work." I'd round up my boy cousins, assign them to different "desks" around my grandmother's living room, and declare myself the boss. I'd give them adding machines (if you're not familiar, they were calculators with paper rolls that made a glorious clickety-clack sound) and go around checking everyone's receipts. "How much did you sell today?" I'd ask, like I was running a mini sales floor in a pretend business.

Sometimes we played school, and I'd be the teacher too. But the theme was always the same. I was the one organizing, leading, asking questions, and making sense of things. I wasn't playing house. I was running the show.

Back then, I didn't know what any of this meant. I wasn't worried about the best salary or what other people thought of my interests. I was doing what made my heart happy. Now I realize how much it revealed about who I would become.

I ended up in high-tech sales, leading teams and closing big deals, often as the only woman in rooms full of powerful men. Maybe if I had really examined how I played when no one was watching, back before I was concerned about what sounded impressive, I might have seen a path that was a more natural fit for me.

How do you feel when you think about the things you used to love doing as a kid? Does it make your heart come alive? Was there a seed of truth about who you were meant to be at a young age? It's worth going back to look at what the little girl version of you loved with adult eyes to see if it's something worth pursuing.

Of course, childhood play doesn't always translate into a neat and tidy list of career options. So when my Plan A didn't pan out, I had to start listening for different clues.

When the Dream Shifts but the Core Stays the Same

I always *thought* I'd be a reporter, so when that didn't work out as expected, I didn't know what was next. I knew I needed to find something more aligned with my identity. Journalism was in the College of Communications, so I decided to see if other fields within that college might be a better fit.

I became curious about how else I could use the skills I enjoyed most from my journalism days, like asking questions and telling stories. Out of the options, advertising seemed the closest to what I was looking for. They asked questions and told stories about businesses, products, and services.

It was an educated guess, but I was onto something. When I got a position at an advertising agency in Austin, my job was basically to interview clients about complicated software products they were selling.

- *Who is it for?*
- *What does it do?*
- *When will they use it?*
- *Why does it matter?*
- *How will it make their life easier?*

I got to ask thousands of questions to make sure advertising connected the business with customers it could truly help.

That curiosity lit me up. I loved digging to find the truth beneath the surface and making that information click for someone else. The role had changed, yet the core passion below the surface was the same. I didn't stay in advertising. Now I see that it was the connective tissue between my Career 1 as a reporter and my Career 2—the one I've been in ever since.

That exposure to the corporate world and my work with software clients led me to high-tech sales. Many of the skills I used in journalism and advertising transferred to this new career. Only now, instead of asking a client about software features, I was asking people about their problems.

- *What's not working?*
- *What are your top priorities?*
- *What's keeping you up at night?*
- *How can I help?*

The truth is, my "reporter" dream never really died; it shape-shifted. In all of the careers I pursued, the common thread was the same: I wanted to get to the heart of the matter. I genuinely wanted to hear the story of the person sitting across from me, ask the right questions, and find the best ways to deliver what they actually needed. I never would have known it when I started out, but these skills are crucial in sales.

Find What Fuels You

Curiosity has always been at my core. For you, it might be nurturing, and you were the little girl taking care of your baby dolls. Maybe it was beauty, and you were the one covered head to toe in paint. You could have loved teaching, animals, building with blocks, or taking toys apart and putting them back together.

It could have been something totally atypical for a child—just look at me! I played "business" from the time I was little until I started working. In high school, I wore khakis, cropped my hair short, and carried a briefcase like a mini businesswoman!

This may sound silly, but try to uncover your "core." It's that steady desire your heart returns to, no matter how much your roles and interests have shifted over the years.

Sometimes your core shows up in a straightforward, linear career path. Lucky you! More often, it zigzags. But it's always there, and you can get creative with how you explore it. That doesn't mean you've failed. It means you're learning more about who you are and applying that information instead of staying stuck on a path that does not fit. That takes guts.

I never would have guessed that my truth-seeking nature would lead me to a successful career in tech sales. Becoming a reporter makes more sense on paper, right? But sometimes, the detour *is* the destination, and the path that doesn't look perfect on a résumé turns out to be the perfect fit for who you are.

Instead of asking yourself what job you should do, maybe the better question is, "What part of me is asking to be expressed in this season of life?"

> INSTEAD OF ASKING YOURSELF WHAT JOB YOU SHOULD DO, MAYBE THE BETTER QUESTION IS, "WHAT PART OF ME IS ASKING TO BE EXPRESSED IN THIS SEASON OF LIFE?"

Now, what if you've looked for that thread and still feel like you're grasping at straws? That's OK too.

If You're Still Figuring It Out

Not everyone gets the luxury of turning their passion into a paycheck, at least not right away. Maybe you're stuck in a job that sucks, and you've got bills to pay. Maybe you've never pinpointed that core passion. Many of us can't "find the thing we love" and make it happen right away. If that's you, I see you. You're not doing anything wrong.

There are still things you can do to find work that feels like you. Start by getting curious. What did you love doing as a kid? What compliments do you hear most often about your skills? Is there an activity you could immerse yourself in so intensely that when you look up, you're shocked at how much time has passed?

Look at your current work too. What do you enjoy, even a little? What do you dread? Try something new, like a class, a hobby, a volunteer role, or a side gig. Pay attention to how you feel, and ask yourself *why* you feel that way.

The things that drain or delight you aren't just surface-level preferences. They're important clues worth following, no matter how small or insignificant they might seem on the surface. The tiniest sparks of joy are trying to light your path and lead you somewhere better. If you're not seeing them yet, consider that hints don't always come from within. Sometimes, the best mirror is someone who knows you well.

Let Your People Tell You What They See in You

My middle son, Graham, has always been deeply compassionate. When he was little, we noticed he was unusually gentle and loving toward animals. We pointed it out frequently and told him he would be a great veterinarian one day. Fast forward to today, and he's in vet school.

Sometimes, other people see things in you long before you recognize them yourself. If you're a parent, this is one of the most powerful gifts you can give your kids: notice their nature. Help them imagine how their unique strengths could shape their future.

As adults, people don't often tell us what they see in us. It can help to ask! Try asking a few close friends, mentors, and colleagues what they think you're naturally good at. Send this text:

"Hey, I'm doing some career reflection and need your help. What's something you think I'm naturally good at? No pressure. I'm curious to see what patterns show up!"

We actually did something similar in my family one Christmas, and it turned out to be one of the most meaningful gift exchanges we've ever done.

We each drew one family member's name and instead of buying gifts for that person, we had to ask *them* for something. The catch: The gift couldn't be tied to money. Instead, we requested a gift from the person whose name we drew based on the natural talents and strengths we saw in them.

My uncle drew my name and asked me to give him my time to help him come up with a few dressy outfits for special occasions. He admired my sense of style and wanted my help looking sharp. I drew my grandmother's name and asked her to record all of her recipes onto cassette tapes so I could always have her voice and her cooking wisdom with me.

The whole experience was beautiful and not only because of the gifts we received, but also because of the rare insights we gained. We got to learn the strengths our family members saw in us but might not think to say out loud. That reminder of the good we bring into the world was an additional gift we each gained.

If you've already identified your unique strengths, don't stop there. Tell someone younger than you what you see in them. You never know who might need to hear it or how much sooner they might step into their calling because you said something out loud.

Coming Home to Yourself

We don't always choose the most aligned career the first time and who can blame us? We're still children when we're asked to pick the path we'll pour our time, energy, and resources into for decades to come—without fully understanding the return.

Don't let unrealistic expectations keep you stuck in a job that's draining you because you've already invested so much in it. Give yourself permission to let your career be a winding road instead of a straight line, even if it means taking some wrong turns before you find the right direction.

Consult the little girl inside of you. How did she naturally think, lead, create, or care for others? What made her feel the most alive before she was concerned with impressing other people or choosing something practical?

You could be a CEO, a stay-at-home mom, or retired. It's still worth pausing to ask: Is what I'm doing now still a fit for who I've become? And if not, what might be calling me next?

No matter your age or your title, you deserve to spend your days doing something that feels right to you in this season of life. You may not have had all the tools to choose the right path the first time around, but it's never too late to find the best direction from here.

> **YOU MAY NOT HAVE HAD ALL THE TOOLS TO CHOOSE THE RIGHT PATH THE FIRST TIME AROUND, BUT IT'S NEVER TOO LATE TO FIND THE BEST DIRECTION FROM HERE.**

CHAPTER 6
The Path You Chose

Am I doing this because I want to or because I have to?

When I graduated from high school, it felt like women had two options: be a "career woman" or a stay-at-home mom. Door number one, you put on a blazer and went to work. Or door number two, you kept your house spotless and became a room mom at your kids' school. In my family, there was no debate. I knew exactly which category I belonged in—I was a career woman.

My grandma worked on an assembly line in the 1960s. My mom balanced ledgers at the bank and then went into sales. I was stuffing envelopes for our family business at 9 years old. Inventory and sales were regular topics around my childhood dinner table. By the time I turned 18, I had fully embraced the tradition: We are a family of working women.

I'll be honest with you here. Back then, I secretly thought the stay-at-home mom door was the "easy way out." I pictured them lounging around in their perfect homes, casually folding laundry while watching soap operas. I wondered, *How could this be fulfilling? How and why would you want to depend on a man to take care of you?*

Turns out, I was dead wrong. There is no "easy" path for most women in this world.

What Do You Mean You Don't Bake Homemade Sourdough?

No matter which path we take as women, life has a way of smacking us with expectations we didn't sign up for. It'll slam you into the mud, demand you get back up, and still expect you to keep the world spinning for everyone around you.

WHAT DO YOU MEAN YOU DON'T BAKE HOMEMADE SOURDOUGH?

The expectations only grow more extreme.

It's not enough to make the cutest Valentines for your kids' friends anymore. Now stay-at-home moms are on social media grinding their own flour, baking sourdough from scratch, raising chickens, growing their own food, and getting paid six figures through brand sponsorships. Meanwhile, corporate women are expected to break glass ceilings and still somehow make it to every soccer game with organic, homemade snacks.

Society keeps raising the bar, and women keep meeting it, proving again and again that we are resourceful, resilient, and endlessly capable. But as we rise to these new expectations, we unintentionally set the bar higher. Our lives are so full that we don't have time to look around and ask ourselves: *Who's making these rules? Do we really want to keep playing this game?*

I didn't fully realize how much these labels box women in until I went on a sales incentive trip while seven months pregnant.

One of our most senior executives, Bob, introduced me to his wife. She smiled at my belly and asked, "So are you a worker or a wife?" That question jarred me. Can women only be one of those things? If I can only be one, which am I? I thought for a second, then looked her right in the eye and said, "I am actually a wife, a worker, *and* a mom. How about that?"

I was, and still am, very proud to be all three of those things. It's the life I chose, and I've worked damn hard for it. But I'm not here to tell women to do more. Instead, no matter which path you've chosen, let's talk honestly about what it takes to show up, speak up, and push forward in a world that keeps demanding more from us.

Finding Your Way in a Man's World

The Austin tech boom of the mid-1990s felt like a huge career opportunity I shouldn't pass up. Not once did I stop to consider the fact that the industry was male dominated and what that might mean for me. The only thing on my mind was proving that going through the "career woman" door was the right choice.

In my first sales job, there was a fairly even mix of men and women on my team. It wasn't until I started climbing the corporate ladder that I noticed fewer women in the room with me. At the leadership level, it often felt like 80% men and 20% women at best. One meeting made the imbalance impossible to ignore. There were 12 men around a conference table, all with Harvard or MIT class rings, and one woman: me.

When I walked into that meeting, there were only a couple of seats left at the table, so I took one. That's a statement I'd tell any career woman to make. Don't park yourself against the wall because you're the only woman.

But as these men started talking, their conversation might as well have been in Mandarin. I couldn't understand a word, and to be honest, that intimidated the hell out of me.

That night, I drove home and called my dad.

"Dad, I'm going to have to go back to school and get a master's degree from Harvard to keep up with these people."

My dad listened as my worries bubbled to the surface. But over the course of that conversation, he helped me come to the conclusion that I didn't need to speak *their* language. I needed to recognize the value that *I* brought to that room. In a meeting full of brilliant engineers, my unique strength was connecting their ideas about voice, the customers' voice, and the business's goals. Without someone there to translate their initiatives into everyday human language, the smartest products in the world would still fail.

At the time, I just thought seeing things in terms of value to the customer and the business was common sense. It's how I was used to operating, so it felt natural to me, like something everyone else in that room probably already understood. But they didn't. That was my unique perspective, and it was a crucial factor in making the product they were building successful.

It took me too long to realize that the skills that come naturally are often our greatest strengths. If I'd owned my unique value years earlier, I wouldn't have been afraid to speak up. I could have seized more opportunities and shown up with more confidence, even in those daunting rooms surrounded by smart male engineers.

That's why I started a business all about helping young professional women identify their superpowers early, so they can walk into any room empowered to use those strengths to

IF YOU'VE BEEN INVITED TO THE TABLE, YOU'RE THERE FOR A REASON.

their advantage. If you've been invited to the table, you're there for a reason. Uncover what only you can bring and lead from that place. (If you want my support figuring that out, get in touch at therealrobingoad.com. I'd love to help!)

Make Noise About What You Want

Early in my career, when I worked at Dell, I wanted a promotion to a regional sales director role that opened up. When a colleague got the job, I felt confused. I knew I was the best candidate, so why did this guy land the position over me? Instead of wallowing, I decided to ask my boss what happened.

"Why didn't you consider me for the regional sales director position?"

His response floored me.

"I didn't know you wanted it."

GASP. What! How did he not know?

Despite all my hard work and all the extra hours I'd put in, I realized I'd never actually said I wanted the role aloud to anyone. I thought my performance would speak for itself. But people can't read your mind. They won't help you fulfill desires you never make known. Closed mouths don't get fed. They don't get promotions either.

The Unexpected Gifts of Speaking Up

A few years later, I had another opportunity to speak up for myself. This time it was over a commission dispute. I had earned a massive commission by hitting every goal in the comp plan and maxing it out. The check I was owed had two zeros and one comma more than what they wanted to pay. I'd followed the rules to the letter, yet they offered me a fraction of what I was due.

I could've let it go. I could've convinced myself that pushing back wasn't worth the risk. But I'd already learned the hard way what happens when you stay quiet. So I decided to escalate the issue to the head of the public sector at Dell at the time, Brian.

I presented the facts, made my case, and…

I didn't get the money.

But I did get something more valuable. Brian became my mentor and sponsor at Dell. Because I spoke up and made sure the right people were aware of what was happening, I earned the trust of someone who would go on to open doors for me that I couldn't open on my own. People knew me as "Brian's gal," and my reputation started to build across departments.

Later on, a director was building out a new partner-channel business in Dell Federal. I was working in a different part of the business, but he came to me to discuss leading this new venture with the goal of deepening relationships with the federal government. Keep in mind that Michael Dell's book, *Be Direct*, is 180 degrees opposite of a partner-centric business model. So this was breaking company culture.

During our conversation, the director brought up the fact that I was mentored by Brian. Maybe he approached me because he thought I might share Brian's views on this complete shift in mental model. Maybe he thought, "If the head of our entire multibillion-dollar business gives this gal time, I should too." I don't know. But I got the job, and I spent the next five years building a $7 billion business.

That experience taught me not to be afraid to stand up for what matters to you. You won't always get exactly what you're asking for, and that's OK. You may not always get what you fought for, but there might be a win, whether in the trust you earn during the process or the reputation that follows you.

The Seven-Minute Window

Getting ahead isn't always about speaking up. Sometimes, it's recognizing when a rare opportunity is staring you in the face and taking advantage of it. Once, I had a meeting with a customer in Florida and the senior vice president of our business area would be joining. We both flew into Orlando at the same time, and we ended up on a 45-minute car ride together to the customer's office.

I could have been nervous. I could have made small talk about the weather. Instead, I saw it for what it was: a 45-minute, uninterrupted one-on-one meeting with a senior executive.

I knew the first impression I made would set the tone. It would either be an awkward, forgettable car ride, or one where I could gain wisdom, build my reputation, and provide some value. So I used the first seven minutes to ask the boldest question I could muster.

"Bill," I said, "You're the highest-ranking person in our business, and you're maybe seven years older than me. I know you haven't outworked me. You haven't outperformed me. We've had similar jobs and worked in similar roles…"

He leaned in, curious where I was going with this, I'm sure.

I continued, "What did you do so right, and what did I do so wrong that you are leading the entire organization, and I'm still a sales exec, in the same job you had 20 years ago?"

This could have backfired on me, but Bill smiled. He told me that he loved the question, and he was glad I asked. Then, he gave me two pieces of advice I'll never forget. First, he told me the first seven years in the technology industry are like dog years. In some industries, each day is like drinking from a fire hose. You learn a lot very quickly, and if you don't get chewed up and spit out in the process, you can progress in your career very quickly too. The seven years Bill had on me allowed him to accelerate quickly up the ranks of IBM.

Timelines are often arbitrary. Put your blinders up, tune out, and focus on your goals.

Bill's second piece of advice was to get clear on a plan. When he first entered the corporate world at 23, he looked up the chain of command and decided which role he wanted one day. In his first one-on-one with his bosses, he told them he wanted to be the CEO of IBM. They both laughed. But it let them know that he was serious about his future with the company. So together, the three of them mapped out a plan to make him VP by a certain age.

See what you want, work backward, make a plan, and make it known.

From experiences like this and many others, I came up with my "seven-minute rule." Never waste the first seven minutes you get with a leader. A fleeting moment with a senior leader is your audition tape, so use it wisely. It's your chance to tap into their hard-won insight *and* plant your own flag. Show you're listening for the lessons and make sure you stand out with your unique vision.

Here's the best part: That seven-minute window can create new opportunities no matter how far you are in your career. In fact, I got my most recent promotion from a seven-minute conversation that almost didn't happen.

I was visiting the Washington, DC office of Amazon Web Services (AWS), the company I currently work for, when my colleague said, "Hey, Robin. I want to take you upstairs to meet Rishi, the new leader around here. He may not be available to chat, but this way, you'll know where his office is, so you can say hi when you're in town."

We walked up to his office and by sheer luck, he wasn't on a call. That alone is rare enough in my world to feel like divine timing.

We shook hands and he said, "I've heard great things about you. Tell me what you do."

"Oh you know, it's not rocket science," I said, and I proceeded to give a quick overview of my work, nothing fancy, just the short version of what I do. In a nutshell, the team assigns me a new project, tells me to go figure it out, and I come up with industry solutions to tackle it. I've developed a nuanced set of skills over decades in the tech industry that I now recognize are my "corporate superpowers."

When I finished my spiel, Rishi looked at me with an enthusiasm I didn't expect.

He said, "Robin, I've been at this company for nine months. This whole time, I've been trying to talk to somebody about everything you just articulated in," he looked down at his watch, "seven minutes!"

He continued, "I have a meeting now, but ask my assistant to book you some time on my calendar for next week. I want you to do everything you just said across my entire global organization."

I was promoted within the week, and that's not the only opportunity I got as a result of that seven-minute window. We did everything I told Rishi we'd do, and eight months later, he nominated me for a leadership program with Matt Garman, the CEO of AWS.

Sometimes, all it takes is a valuable seven-minute conversation to alter your career trajectory. If you can clearly communicate your value, you can open doors that might otherwise take years to knock down. After that comes the real test: You have to back up your word with action. That chain of events brought me back to something I'd heard about career success years earlier. It was a piece of advice so simple I almost dismissed it.

What's the Secret to Success?

When Dell flew in a keynote speaker for our Women in Tech Excellence event one year, we all expected meaningful insights into how we could excel in this industry. Maybe a playbook for the coming year or a detailed blueprint for personal growth. I sat down, pen and paper in hand, ready to take pages of notes.

Instead, the speaker made a statement that was almost too simple.

He tapped the mic and asked the room, "What's the secret to success?"

"Know what you're good at, and do what you say you're going to do."

There was a moment of pause in the room. You could almost hear us collectively thinking to ourselves, *Is that it?* He seemed to anticipate this reaction. He smiled and proceeded to clarify his point.

"Do you know how many people literally don't do what they say they're going to do? Eighty percent. If you make a point to stay true to your word, you're already in the top twenty percent of the population."

Mind-blowing. This concept felt a bit like a corporate fortune cookie at first. But I started thinking about the people I'd worked with over the years. It actually *was* rare for the average person to consistently stay true to their word on things as small as replying to an email "by end of day" or as significant as hitting a big project deadline promised months in advance.

Follow through was a common trait among those who rose in the ranks. It felt like a no-brainer to me, but it was a lightbulb moment. Because something seems obvious to you doesn't mean it's obvious, or easy, for everyone else. What feels natural to one person might be the exact thing another struggles to grasp or doesn't realize they're missing.

I'm proud to have had a very successful career, and at this stage, I see how much success *does* come down to the basics. Flashy credentials and complicated frameworks don't get you ahead on their own.

I can distill my success down to a few traits that may feel obvious, like that speaker's advice did to me at first. Intentionally building these characteristics could be the difference between staying where you are and getting to where you want to go.

1. **Curiosity:** You can't be successful at something you're not interested in. Make a real effort to learn about your customers, your company, and how the business actually works. The best career moves I made came from asking better questions, not from having all the answers.

2. **Fearlessness:** You don't get promoted for staying quiet. Every big step forward in my career started with a moment where I showed up, spoke up, and let myself be seen, even when it was uncomfortable.

3. **Problem-solving:** Whatever your job is, it likely comes down to solving a problem for other people. Instead of focusing on a list of tasks, zoom out and think about the problem you solve. Determine how you can do a better job of listening, figuring out what's broken, and fixing it. Proactive problem-solving makes you memorable to decision makers.

4. **Discernment:** It takes the same amount of energy to win a $500 million deal as it does a $5 million deal. Get good at determining which opportunities are worth your time, and use your energy and resources accordingly.

These skills have been crucial for me over the past several decades. But there's another one that might matter more than all the others combined. It's the trait that's powered every promotion, partnership, and multimillion-dollar deal across my entire career. I'm still shocked by how rare it is.

You Have to Genuinely Give a Shit About People

A while back, AWS paid a hefty sum to a consulting firm so they could teach my sales team…basic empathy. They rolled into Austin with talks prepared on things like

> **I SAT IN THE BACK ROW THINKING, CARING ABOUT OTHERS IS NOW A BILLABLE SKILL WE HAVE TO TRAIN PEOPLE ON. LORD, HELP US.**

"active listening." I sat in the back row thinking, *caring about others is now a billable skill we have to train people on. Lord, help us.*

Not long after, I was on a flight listening to one of my favorite podcasts, *The Mel Robbins Podcast*. She was interviewing Dr. Alison Wood Brooks from Harvard Business School about her book, *Talk: The Science of Conversation and the Art of Being Ourselves*. Brooks shared that great negotiators don't start with their own agenda, even if what they're negotiating is a raise or promotion. They start with the other person's best interests in mind.

You could practically hear Mel's jaw hit the floor. She said, "I never thought of it that way." As a former lawyer, she admitted she'd spent her career approaching negotiations like a courtroom where she had to "win her case." And for her to win, the person on the other side of the table had to lose.

Once again, I thought this was a given to everyone in the working world. As the interview played out in my earbuds, my first instinct was to think to myself, *how many people are just now realizing this? We're really teaching this at Harvard?*

I didn't go to Harvard Business School, but I must have picked up this Ivy League lesson at the start of my career. Over 30 successful years in tech sales, I *never* approached a conversation with the primary goal of "winning" a sale. My goal is to learn the client's problems and ask enough questions to find out how one of the solutions in my toolbox might help. If I can help, great! If I can't help, no harm, no foul. Maybe you'll remember me when you need the support I have to offer.

Career success is about relationships, not transactions. I don't care how strong your résumé is. If people don't feel like you care about them, they won't follow you, they won't advocate for you behind closed doors, and they won't buy what you're selling. Period.

> **IF PEOPLE DON'T FEEL LIKE YOU CARE ABOUT THEM, THEY WON'T FOLLOW YOU, THEY WON'T ADVOCATE FOR YOU BEHIND CLOSED DOORS, AND THEY WON'T BUY WHAT YOU'RE SELLING. PERIOD.**

You could be meeting a client, a colleague, or a top executive at your company. It doesn't matter. Walk into the room and genuinely care about the person sitting across from you. Put yourself in their shoes. Take the time to understand what they really need not in business terms, but at the core. What's keeping them up at night? What are their top three priorities this quarter, and how can your team help? Heck, what sports do their kids play?

Most people come to all conversations thinking about how to get what they want and how they're being perceived. The best way to achieve a favorable outcome is to do the opposite. Show up with a curious mindset. Ask better questions. Listen without rushing to speak. Make it about them.

This isn't a trick. When it's actually authentic, people feel it. So that's my career fortune cookie for you: You don't have to be the smartest person in the room. You don't need a Harvard class ring on your finger. But you do need to care. Because you can't build a meaningful career, or a meaningful life, if you don't give a shit about the people in it.

CHAPTER 7

What You Really Want

What do you want? Such a simple question,
but so hard to answer.

A coworker of mine, Carol, gave our corporation 12 long, hard years. Flying redeyes, managing teams, and clocking extra hours every week. In an industry known to chew up and spit out even the highest achievers, she thrived, and she made a big impact in our department. But finally, she decided to move on.

On Carol's last day, she boxed up the plastic plants and family photos from her desk, dropped her badge off with security, and left the building. There was no goodbye party. The only acknowledgment of her departure was a three-line email.

Before the day ended, her team was divided up between me and two other leaders. Carol's name wasn't mentioned in a team meeting the following week. She had made some incredible achievements for our company in the same role as me, and it was like she never worked there.

I wish I could tell my 30-year-old self that *that* is the moment waiting for you at the top of every career ladder. On some level, we all understand that we won't get to our deathbeds wishing we'd gone to more meetings. But as women in the corporate world, we still so easily slip into caring too much. Our relationship with work *should* be balanced and mutually beneficial, yet we often give way more than we receive, regardless of the number on our paycheck.

Carol's story was a wake-up call for me. Work should never be something you give your whole life to. At the end of the day, you're replaceable to your company. And you'll never get back the time you've been given on this earth.

I've always been an overachiever, but lately, I'm thinking less about work accomplishments. My thought process is starting to look more like this: *Work is a means to an end, but what end exactly? What are you chasing, Robin? What pursuit would be worth the energy you give to your work every day?*

For me and so many women I know, the career "high" is real. The praise, the paycheck, and the feeling of being needed hooked me early. Work gave me something I didn't know how to give myself: proof that I mattered.

I didn't question how much I depended on work to support my self-worth or how much I willingly gave up to get that fix—until it started to wear off.

When the Career "Drug" Wears Off

When my husband, Shannon, was in the army, they told him he was the perfect soldier because he didn't have a close-knit family. That allowed him to focus harder on his unit.

To corporate America, a broken little girl is the perfect soldier.

I say this with compassion, not judgment, because I've been that girl. Hell, I made a career out of being that girl. Now that I'm in my 50s looking back on my career, I can see that my trauma and baggage made me an ideal fit for the corporate world.

Broken little girls become women who will break their backs to prove themselves in the workplace. They give 200% day in and day out without questioning it. The more broken they are, the more successful they become because they're that much more driven to earn approval, validation, and the sense of belonging that was missing growing up.

When there's a vacuum of purpose and meaning in your life, not only will work fill it, you'll be rewarded generously for giving work everything you've got. Your higher-ups will be happy to see you put your career on a pedestal above all else. That praise feels *good*, so you keep going. In most cases, no one in your professional circle will try to stop you from pouring every last drop of your time and energy into work.

If I'd been a balanced human at 25, I might have established healthier professional habits like working 40 hours a week, making the most of my benefits, and heading home to live a life. Instead, I logged 60 (sometimes up to 90) hours per week because I couldn't stop myself.

My father retired at 65, and I saw firsthand the consequences of living this way. He got sick at 69, and how many people from work came to visit him in the hospital? Zero.

When I sat at his bedside and looked around, I saw a room full of family and friends. No one from my dad's professional life came even once to wish him well. My dad passed away just four years after he retired.

That shook me. I saw how easy it is to give your best years to a job that will never love you like your people do. The career high doesn't last forever. At some point, the praise goes quiet and you're left asking yourself, *was that really worth everything I gave it?*

> **THE CAREER HIGH DOESN'T LAST FOREVER. AT SOME POINT, THE PRAISE GOES QUIET AND YOU'RE LEFT ASKING YOURSELF, WAS THAT REALLY WORTH EVERYTHING I GAVE IT?**

Today, I believe that a paycheck should be a *means* to an end, not the *meaning* of your life. I hope you realize this sooner than I did. Because the hard truth is that at the end of your life, you'll either be surrounded by the people you invested in or painfully aware of the ones you didn't.

Rewiring your priorities is easier said than done, I know. The first step is getting honest about where your energy actually goes.

Your Mouth, Your Money, Your Month

One time, I heard a preacher talk about the three Ms—your mouth, your money, and your month—as a tool for gaining clarity on your priorities. Here's how he explained it.

- **Your mouth**: What do you spend your time talking about? If I were a fly on the wall for the conversations you have throughout the day, what I heard you speak about would tell me exactly what your priorities are.

- **Your money:** What do you spend your money on? If you were to show me your recent bank statements and look at what you spend your money on, that would tell me what you value most.
- **Your month:** What do you spend your time on over the course of a month? If I were to open up your calendar and look at the appointments, meetings, events, and everything you spend your days doing, that would tell me what's most important to you.

Then to go deeper and ask yourself how present you are for the events and obligations penciled onto your calendar. When you're at your kid's basketball game, do you sit there and watch, or are you on your phone replying to work emails?

If your answers don't match up with what you *want* to prioritize in your life, now is a great time to ask how you can adjust. Your mouth, your money, and your month are the most valuable currency you possess. How you spend them should be a conscious decision. If someone had told me that years ago, I would've taken off work to chaperone more field trips while my kids were little.

This reflection may help you realize you're already living in alignment with your priorities, and you should cut yourself some slack. Others may need to make a few minor changes. But for some, you may find that your current career doesn't align with what you want for your life. Don't ignore that feeling. Lean in.

Career Crossroads: Pivot or Adjust?

Figuring out what truly fulfills you doesn't happen overnight. Sometimes, the things that bring the most meaning to your life start as random experiments.

Take my mother-in-law, Maudie. She quit school in sixth grade and worked in a cafeteria at a tire plant in Arizona. She and her husband worked 40 hours a week. But then they'd go home, make a sandwich, and head out to renovate properties together. They bought one rental property at a time, fixing them up and learning as they went.

At 93 years old, Maudie still owns 12 rental properties. She loves taking care of those properties, and she turned that side project into something that could sustain her for life. Decades after buying her first property, she still drives around, picks up her rental checks, and enjoys the fruits of a decision she made long ago.

Imagine if she'd never taken the time to explore anything outside of work. Her entire future would've looked different.

You don't need a full-blown plan today. You just need enough space on your calendar to lean into the things that give you energy. One of those activities for me is hosting. I can spend a weekend hosting my son Spencer's entire baseball team, preparing food, cooking, and cleaning, and not feel tired.

Explore the things you can do for eight hours straight and not get tired. You could learn that it isn't for you after all, or it could become a viable career path. Either way, you won't have a lingering "what if" at the back of your mind if you give it an honest try.

If your career no longer fits, it doesn't mean you failed. It means you're paying attention. If you're able to leap, then leap. If you can't yet, then plan. Ask where you want to be in two or three years, then work backward. What skills would help? What financial buffer would you need to feel secure?

Your most aligned career path won't emerge overnight. But small, consistent actions can get you closer to your goal. Just like my Maudie, you can build something meaningful with a few extra hours per week.

Time will pass either way. The question is whether it's carrying you toward the life you want. That's not something I asked myself until I was in my 50s, and to be honest, I *never* would have expected my priorities to shift the way they have.

Legacy Beyond the Résumé

After decades of chasing the next rung on the ladder, I'm now less interested in achievements. The more interesting question to me these days is, "Who can I help?"

It's a shame for women to get older and decide their insights don't matter anymore. We've spent a lifetime collecting hard-won wisdom. Why wouldn't we use it to open doors for others? Giving back in this way isn't only good for the people you help, it can be incredibly fulfilling for you too.

Once, at a corporate dinner, I sat next to a guy named Chris who worked in a different department. I learned that he was an attorney who'd served in the military for 20 years, yet he held a surprisingly junior role at our company. I was shocked that he was flying under the radar.

After that night, I started dropping Chris's name in rooms he wasn't in and telling people how talented he was. Before long, he made it onto our company's top talent list. I was so proud of the impact I had on his journey.

Sponsoring, mentoring, and lifting others up is the part of my work that I love most now. It makes my career mean something beyond my own success. The people I vouch for will go on to do bigger things, and I'll know I had a hand in that.

Nothing beats knowing your impact will have a ripple effect on the lives of others long after you're gone. But here's another important thing to keep in mind. No matter how many times you've been around the block, there is always more to learn.

Will You Keep Growing? It's Up to You

No matter how old you are, if you're a career woman or a stay-at-home mom, remember that it's never too late to learn new things.

I've seen it too many times where people reach a certain age or level in their career and stop learning. They assume they've already figured it all out. They stop pushing themselves, asking questions, and allowing others to introduce them to new ideas.

It's easy to get comfortable in what you know. But the most fulfilled people I know are the ones who've made a point to keep learning and challenging themselves, whether they're in their 20s or their 70s.

Picking up new lessons in life keeps us young, makes us interesting to others, and gives our lives more meaning right up to the end. So stay curious and find new ways to push yourself in your career and your life. Make mistakes, ruffle some feathers, and decide today to never stop growing.

What Really Matters

Growth is a funny thing. Most of us start our careers trying to become someone new: a more skilled, polished, and impressive version of ourselves. But if we're lucky, all

> **BUT IF WE'RE LUCKY, ALL THAT STRIVING BRINGS US HOME TO THE MOST IMPORTANT LESSON. THE GREATEST GIFT YOU HAVE TO GIVE IS YOUR AUTHENTIC SELF.**

that striving brings us home to the most important lesson. The greatest gift you have to give is your authentic self.

For many of us, authenticity isn't our first instinct. We suppress who we are and the things we love to achieve someone else's idea of success. But now that I'm 30 years into my sales career, I'm finally ready to embrace the authentic core of who I am: the little girl who wanted to tell stories, ask tough questions, and help people find the truth.

A truth I've realized is that the most important aspect of your career isn't what you achieve. It's who is by your side when the achievements stop. And the good news is, even if you don't know *what* your most authentic self should do with her life yet, you can work on *how* she'd show up starting today.

I'm good at what I do, and yet I have never once felt like a salesperson.

I tell customers that my goal is to see you in an airport in 20 years and not have to run and hide. I want to run up to you and hug your neck. Funny enough, I had the opportunity to do that once.

I saw a former client, Mr. Williams, at the airport. I walked up and enthusiastically greeted him like an old friend, only to discover that he had no idea who I was. Turns out, Mr. Williams has a twin brother!

Once we figured it out, we texted the real Mr. Williams, and the three of us had a good laugh. His twin told me, "There are worse things than having a beautiful blonde woman confuse me for my brother with a hug! At least you weren't a bill collector!"

I'd rather risk hugging the wrong person than have people remember me as cold or transactional. I'd rather be someone who makes people feel appreciated and seen.

That's how I show up authentically. How about you?

- How do you want people to feel after spending time with you?
- What kind of presence do you hope to bring into the room?
- Do you show up in a way that reflects your true values?

No matter what you do in your career, whether it's your dream job or something to fund your real passions, what really matters is how you showed up, how you made people feel, and your true connections when it's all said and done. Prioritize those things, and you can't go wrong.

PART 2 REFLECTION: TIME TO GET REAL

Before you move on, take a moment to pause and reflect on this part of your life. The questions below are here to help you get honest with yourself.

You can journal your answers, talk them out with a friend, or simply sit with them for a bit. But don't be afraid to go deeper than you usually would. Slowing down long enough to really look at your life can help you understand yourself better, make meaningful changes, and become the woman you're meant to be.

1. Do you have any childhood career dreams you might want to revisit? Could you make a living doing it? What would it look like to explore that dream today?
2. Do you have a sponsor who could help you get more from your career? Can you ask someone you admire if they'd be willing to mentor you or meet for coffee?
3. If no one judged your answer, what do you really want next in your work life? What's one small move you could make toward that desire in the next month?

> If you're a young professional woman navigating corporate America, don't make the same mistake I made. I thought performing and achieving at a high level would be enough to get ahead, but it's not.

You wouldn't walk onto a football field or into a war zone without knowing the rules and having a strategy to win. So why show up to work without one?

After 30 years in the corporate world, I'd love to help you strategize your path to corporate success. I help women like you learn the unwritten rules, find hidden opportunities, and create a strategic plan for reaching goals. If that sounds like the next step for you, visit therealrobingoad.com to reach out and let's start the conversation.

PART 3
Your Health

Women are beautifully complex creatures.
Made that way for a reason.

Every now and then, my husband teases me by saying something like, "Women are just *that way*." I laugh and tell him to hush. But I know he's right.

As women, we *are* emotional. We *are* spiritual. We go through physical shifts and challenges that men don't. And you know what? That's nothing to be ashamed of. It's one of the great miracles of being a woman. (We're the givers of life! Could you expect us to be anything *less* than complicated?)

In fact, thank God we're made the way we are. The world would be too black and white without our femininity. Women provide our society with care, nurturing, creativity, intuition, and warmth that we wouldn't have otherwise. But here's the thing: We have to keep ourselves healthy, balanced, and functioning well to benefit from these gifts.

Our mental, spiritual, physical, and financial health all work together as a complex ecosystem. When one part suffers, the whole thing can be thrown off course. And when one part begins to heal, it can be enough to change everything.

I see women as fluid creatures. We flow in and out of emotions, seasons, and identities throughout our lives. Our bodies are designed that way, expanding to shelter and nourish another life. I watched my body do that to bring four children into this world. I've been brought to my knees by heartbreak and pain that could've taken me out. And yet, somehow, I survived it all. That's what we're *made* to do.

Remember this when you feel broken: As a woman, your complexity isn't a burden. It's a garden to be tended. It grows all the ingredients you need to shapeshift throughout your life to heal, walk through fire, and chase your wildest dreams. All while showing up as the mother, partner, leader, and friend— the woman you were meant to be.

This is why we need to talk about your health, and not just numbers on a chart, but the full picture. Because this beautifully complex ecosystem is the foundation of your life. Tending to your health isn't only about feeling good or showing up for others. It's how you take care of every version of *you* still to come.

CHAPTER 8

Mental and Emotional Health

*Your past may have planted seeds,
but you get to decide what grows.*

**This chapter includes discussion of trauma, including childhood
sexual abuse and postabortion healing. While the content is
handled with care, please take what you need and skip what you
don't. Your emotional safety matters.*

There's this meme that makes the rounds with a woman
lying in bed with 1,500 thoughts racing through her head.
Maybe she's thinking:

Did I send that email?

What should I make for dinner tomorrow night?

Why did my kid's teacher ask to meet with me?

Meanwhile, her husband lies next to her with just one thought
on his mind:

Are we having sex tonight?

It's funny because for many women, it's so relatable! But when you sit with it, there's something frustrating about this picture. Why are women so often the ones lying awake with the emotional weight of the day?

No one told me how much of womanhood would be about managing what's unseen, the invisible labor, the emotional load, and all of these expectations we never agreed to but somehow inherited anyway. That's probably because no one told the women in the generation before me or the ones before them.

That's why this chapter felt so important to write. I want there to be at least one woman in your life who tells you that checking in with your mental and emotional health isn't optional, indulgent, or a sign of weakness. It's as essential as taking care of your body.

I've listened to tons of podcasts and read countless studies while researching for this book, and I still can't understand why it's like this. Have we always been the ones carrying the bulk of the mental load? Why do we put so much on our shoulders and try to power through it all alone?

For me, that pressure to hold it all together used to show up as the fear of being "found out" for what was really going on in my life. I'd walk into rooms and think, *if they only knew.* If the other moms knew that I'd just signed a multimillion-dollar deal, would they still want to be friends with me? I wanted them to like me and see me as a supermom. I didn't want to intimidate them.

The ladies at my church saw me as the put-together woman who never missed a Sunday. They didn't know I'd been promiscuous when I was young and had three abortions. I was sure if they knew, they'd never look at me the same.

And as a mother, God help me. If my kids knew how often I was making it all up as I went along, that I had no idea what good parenting looked like, would they stop trusting me?

We hide the truth about ourselves because we're afraid of being judged or rejected. But that fear is a cage. It keeps us isolated, stressed, and suffering more than necessary. And when the pressure finally spills over, we don't ask what's wrong with the system. We wonder what's wrong with *us.* That fear becomes emotional labor and eventually, emotional exhaustion.

But here's what makes this conversation so crucial. When you don't address what's going on inside, it affects everything on the outside, including your relationships, energy, joy, work, and ability to cope, persevere, and live well. Your mental health shapes how your days play out, and over time, it shapes the story of your life.

Whatever you're feeling, know that there's another woman out there who could say, "I've been there too." You're not alone, and mental health struggles aren't anything new. We just haven't always had the permission, or the language, to name them.

Mental Health Is Not a New Phenomenon

Mental health isn't new. But sometimes society treats it like a modern issue. Open any historical book, and it won't take long to find commentary around mental health struggles, although the ways we discuss them have changed over time.

Sarah Wesley, wife of the 18th-century Methodist leader Charles Wesley, wrote letters about a friend who was depressed. The preacher Charles Spurgeon battled depression for more than 20 years in the 1800s. Florence Nightingale, the founder of modern nursing, is now believed to have lived with bipolar disorder. St. Teresa of Calcutta wrote that her ministry was marked by depression and deep emotional pain.

Mental and emotional health have impacted people's lives since the beginning of time. But what *is* new is how we're starting to discuss these topics with more nuance. As with physical health, mental health isn't all or nothing. You're not either "fine" or "falling apart." There's a wide range in between. You might be holding joy in one hand and grief in the other. You can feel fine one day and struggle to get out of bed the next.

That's why tending to your mental health daily is so important. That means carving out time for rest, reflection, honest conversations, and community. This is how you recover your energy to survive another day. Without prioritizing your version of mental healthcare, stress compounds and the mind suffers for it.

When I first started paying attention to my mental health, I saw that my inner dialogue shaped how I felt and behaved. I've always been an overachiever, but now I could see the connection between my trauma history and my drive to perform and please. Let me tell you, it may not be your schedule or circumstances wearing you down. It could be the outdated beliefs you have running in the background.

> LET ME TELL YOU, IT MAY NOT BE YOUR SCHEDULE OR CIRCUMSTANCES WEARING YOU DOWN. IT COULD BE THE OUTDATED BELIEFS YOU HAVE RUNNING IN THE BACKGROUND.

Which Beliefs Still Run Your Life?

In chapter 3, I told you about the nervous breakdown I had at my friend's cabin. That's when I realized the false subconscious belief I'd carried since childhood: If my own mother didn't love me enough to protect me from my abusive, alcoholic stepdad, I must be unlovable.

That belief wreaked havoc on my life and relationships until I could finally identify and start unlearning it.

Another false belief from my childhood was the idea that if I performed and people-pleased well enough, the adults in my life could coexist peacefully.

Of course, my stepdad's blow-up fights with my mom weren't within my control. It wasn't my responsibility to keep the adults around me emotionally regulated. But when you're young and trying to make sense of chaos, you'll believe just about anything that helps the world feel a little safer.

Our minds can easily misinterpret lessons, take on lies as the "truth," and let those false beliefs lead us to harmful decisions well into adulthood. In my case, I kept performing to earn appreciation and to avoid conflict in my work and relationships. It took me a long time to realize that pattern, and even longer to undo it.

After I divorced my first and second husbands, I always tried to keep the peace with them. If they called last minute to say they couldn't get the kids from school, I'd drop everything and rearrange my plans so I could pick them up. Keeping the peace felt necessary. But it cost me more than I realized at the time.

Even today, when my adult children ask me to do something, I catch myself wanting so badly to make them happy. Sometimes that means I say yes without considering my needs or bandwidth. It's my first instinct to keep everything "OK," which can still cause me to forget to maintain healthy boundaries.

I have reframed those beliefs by learning how boundaries are a form of self-respect. Not setting them is unfair to me and the people in my life; it's a recipe for resentment. Knowing this truth makes it a little easier to prioritize my mental health because I know it isn't a selfish thing to do. It's healthy. When you tend to your needs, that act of self-kindness helps you nurture others from a place of authenticity rather than obligation.

If you relate to similar patterns, it might be time to ask yourself:

- *Wait, why do I always take care of everyone else first?*
- *Why do I get so uncomfortable with calm and stability?*
- *Why do I keep ending up in the same kind of relationship?*

Start sorting out which beliefs were planted in survival mode and which ones you actually want to grow your life around now. If only I could have ripped out my false beliefs like weeds in a garden *decades* sooner than I did, it would've saved me from deep emotional pain caused by years of destructive behavior.

On Destructive Behavior

Self-destructive behavior stems from unresolved trauma. It could look like harmful behavior, disorders, or addiction to food, sugar, alcohol, relationships, perfectionism, or performance. If you notice patterns like that in yourself, this is a loving invitation to pause, assess what's going on, and find ways to heal.

One of the ways I've found healing is through supporting other women. For years, I've volunteered for a postabortion healing ministry that holds intensive weekend retreats. I've met thousands of women across all generations, and it's eerie how similar our stories are. The women I meet didn't have an abortion because they were weak or reckless. They almost always have some sort of trauma history, and that's true for me too.

In some ways, it feels like I was almost predestined to have an abortion. I was an only child with incredibly high expectations placed on me to be the perfect human. My parents divorced when I was seven, and my mother remarried an abusive alcoholic when I was nine. Then there was the traumatic event that happened when I was four—something I suppressed until decades later.

Around the time I started to wonder about the unhealthy patterns in my first marriage, flashes of a four-year-old girl on a couch began appearing in my mind. The details were fuzzy, but I felt she was somehow connected to the work I needed to do for my mental health.

After I had my daughter, I experienced a moment connected to that little girl on the couch, although I didn't understand it at the time.

One day when I was 25 and Macy was still a baby, I laid her on her changing table. Her doctor had told me to check her temperature using a rectal thermometer. I held her little legs up and felt this overwhelming need to apologize to her.

I said, "Macy, I'm so sorry. I know this is going to hurt." But when I took her temperature, she didn't cry like I expected or notice what I was doing. I realized my brain was having an abnormal reaction to the situation. *The doctor didn't warn me about pain. Why was I so sure that taking her temperature was going to hurt her?*

Back then, I didn't have the answer. I tucked the moment away and moved on. It wasn't until nearly 20 years later, when I began my abortion healing journey, that the memory of that day came back to me with more clarity. That same 4-year-old girl flashed into my mind again, and I realized what she had to do with that strange feeling I had when taking Macy's temperature. That's when I picked up the phone to call my mom.

"Mom, do you remember a house with a big window in the front? There was a gray and yellow plaid sofa in the living room and a silver table in the kitchen. Is that somewhere I went when I was little?"

My mom responded, "You're describing your Aunt Deb's house. But you were so little when I took you there. How do you even remember that?"

I still get goosebumps thinking about how I felt in that moment. My mother's response confirmed it for me. The fragmented story emerging in my mind wasn't some random, recurring daydream. That 4-year-old girl on the plaid couch was me. I remembered it all now. My uncle laid me down there. He told me he was taking my temperature.

That's why I associated Macy's thermometer with pain. Because my uncle hadn't checked my temperature that day. He'd sexually assaulted me.

When I shared this memory with my family, I learned that my uncle had molested another girl in the family, too. No one had ever talked about that, so my mom didn't know not to leave me at his house.

That memory resurfaced about ten years ago, 20 years after that day with Macy, while I was going through my abortion healing journey. It became a turning point in my deeper healing. Three marriages, four children, and countless counseling sessions later, I could finally start connecting the dots.

I went through the same postabortion healing process that I now guide other women through. I told my story in the presence of a nonjudgmental community. I prayed. I allowed myself grieve. I sat with the parts of my past that led to the three abortions I'd had as a teenager and finally pieced together the truth.

I realized that it isn't normal for a 13-year-old girl to want to seduce men and have sex. My whole life, I'd thought that was just me being "bad." I believed all of this was my fault, and I deserved to punish myself for my mistakes forever. There's another lie. The truth was that my trauma led to my self-destructive behavior. It didn't define me; it was something Jesus could heal.

Over time, this work allowed me to shed the shame I'd carried my entire life. It took years, but I can finally talk about my past shame free. I no longer live in fear. I feel whole.

This is why I'm so passionate about helping women start this journey when they're younger, so they don't carry pain for decades or spiral into destructive cycles that derail their future. I thank God that I never became a drug addict or an alcoholic. The drugs I used to numb my pain were performance, pleasing others, and repeating toxic relationship dynamics.

Now that I've done the work, I can see those patterns for what they are. If I meet a woman whose life is unraveling, I don't judge her. I lean in with love and grace and say, "What's going on? What are you running from?"

If you see a woman behaving in a self-destructive way, I promise there's a reason she's doing this to herself. I've seen this pattern play out in hundreds of women's lives.

If that woman is you, consider working with a therapist or trauma counselor. Get the support you need to move forward in your healing journey. Your trauma wasn't your fault, and you shouldn't have to spend your life suffering for it.

Here's a step you can take today that might surprise you, no journaling or meditation required. Instead, tune into your anger. When was the last time you got angry? What makes you mad and why? Your anger can be a powerful compass, pointing to where you need healing most.

What Your Anger Really Means

Anger gets a bad rap, especially for women. We're told to calm down and stop being so "emotional." But sometimes anger is the most honest voice we have. When rage bubbles up, it's not always about the thing that just happened. It could be a reaction to pain you've suppressed or needs that have gone unmet.

What would happen if you saw your anger as helpful data that can support your healing, rather than a personal flaw? It can reveal anything from where your boundaries were crossed to losses you still need to grieve. Here are a few signs that anger is unhealed pain in disguise:

1. **Your voice gets louder when it feels like no one's listening.** You don't want to fight. You're just tired of feeling unheard. You shouldn't have to shout to get your point across or your needs met.
2. **Others describe you as cold or distant.** You want to be joyful around the people you love, but you're drained from holding everything together. You need permission to fall apart and not be "on" for a little while.

3. **You overreact to small things.** If something minimal (like a late reply) makes you angry or brings you to tears, then something deeper is causing that reaction. Healing can start by keeping a few small promises to yourself.
4. **You push people away.** If you snap or say "I'm fine" when you're not, you could be trying to avoid abandonment by rejecting the other person *first*. You need to teach your nervous system that your relationships are safe.
5. **You seem mean or irritable.** You might be living in survival mode after being let down too many times. You need to be around people who can approach you with patience. And you need to be patient with yourself too.

Don't punish yourself for feeling anger. Lean in and ask what it's trying to show you. If you're thinking: "Why do I feel this way all the time lately?" I've got news for you, sister. It might be more than unhealed pain.

Sometimes what feels like rage or depression isn't trauma at all. It's your body changing in ways no one warned you about. Don't kill me, but it could be your hormones screwing with you. Let's have a quick chat about menopause.

Is It Menopause?

Here's the public service announcement I wish I'd received on my 40th birthday: There will come a day when your mental health suddenly feels like it's unraveling for no clear reason. If you feel angry all the time, cry more than usual, or question whether you're losing your mind, it might not be depression. It might be your hormones.

When I was 43, I found myself wanting to lie on the couch all day. My body felt heavy, my brain was foggy, and I'd lost interest in work projects. As a chronic overachiever, this wasn't like me.

Some days I thought I was depressed, other days I thought I was going crazy. But really, someone should've shown up at my door with balloons and a sign that said, "Welcome to perimenopause!"

No one had warned me. I didn't see it coming. But when I finally booked an appointment with my doctor, we decided to move forward with hormone support.

Your mental health issues might indicate something else going on with your body. If you've ruled out trauma and still feel like you're unraveling, don't overlook what your body might be trying to tell you. Don't gaslight yourself. If something feels off, trust your intuition and find a doctor who takes you seriously.

Start by looking at things like your hormone levels before assuming it's all in your mind. As women, we're flooded with chemicals that make us relational when we hit puberty. We're wired to put other people's needs first. We do that for decades, and in this way, menopause is an interesting experience; for the first time in a very long time, our internal voice comes in loud and clear.

I've loved that I'm more able to make decisions for *me* in this stage of life. But my hope for young women is that they can tune into their needs much sooner than menopause. Your inner voice that whispers what would make your life feel like yours again is in there now, no matter your age. You have to pause long enough to hear it.

The Ripple Effect of Living Life for You

We've talked about the false beliefs we adopt as a means of survival, like the one that told me I was unlovable. Well, I bet you have some good beliefs, deep within your soul, that are trying to steer you in the right direction. Those are the kind worth holding onto and handing down.

Toward the end of our marriage, I asked my first husband, "Are you OK living an OK life?"

He didn't hesitate. "Absolutely," he said.

That was when I realized that an "OK" life is good enough for some people. But it isn't for me. I wanted to have the kind of life where you set a family goal each year and work to achieve those goals. You push each other to be better. I wanted a life full of challenges, growth, learning, and feeling alive.

That realization has brought me through several rough patches and helped me avoid living on autopilot. It's helped me make brave decisions and say goodbye to circumstances and relationships that weren't working.

Years after that conversation with my first husband, my daughter Macy was engaged to someone who seemed safe, but I could tell she was settling. She tried hard to convince me that she was in love with him. I didn't buy it.

I asked her, "You've never settled for anything in your life. You wanted to go to the University of Texas, and you found a way.

You wanted to live in NYC, and you found a way. Now because one guy broke your heart, you're going to settle for someone who feels safe?"

She thought about it and eventually broke off the engagement. She realized she wanted a life full of joy, pain, ups and downs, good and bad. She wanted to take risks and seek adventure, not play it safe.

I didn't realize when it was happening, but my daughter saw me stepping out and taking risks. I thought she only saw my flaws and mistakes, and yet she also saw me dreaming big and making those dreams come to life. Despite my low points, I'm proud that my determination to live life on my terms rubbed off on my kids. That's the thing about beliefs—your best ones can support the next generation too.

Girl by Birth, Woman by Fire

Mental and emotional health are no joke. The mind can become a dangerous place if you don't do the work to heal. This stuff doesn't have an end point; you can't tick off boxes and call it a day. It's an ongoing conversation between who you've been and the woman you're becoming.

Most of us come into womanhood with baggage, and some more than others. But these days, I like to see the rough points in my life like the friction that buffs rocks over time. The more friction a rock endures, the more beautiful it becomes.

> **THE MORE FRICTION A ROCK ENDURES, THE MORE BEAUTIFUL IT BECOMES.**

We all start in the soft, safe warmth of our mother's womb, but diamonds aren't forged without immense pressure and heat. Maybe the hell we go through can help us become the most vibrant version of ourselves too. Girl by birth, woman by fire.

I wish we didn't have to experience loss, hardship, suffering, or trauma. But since we do, why not use it as fuel to show up in our lives with fierce power and strength? We can heal. We can control the story from here. Your past may have planted seeds, but you get to decide what grows.

So be gentle with yourself. Keep growing and healing. Let every battle scar be a reminder that no fire you've walked through has burned you down. They've each made you the strong, beautiful woman you are.

CHAPTER 9

Faith, Spirituality, and Meaning

Your faith is the foundation for everything.

The first Sunday of my life, I went to church. My mother bundled me up at seven days old and brought me into that little sanctuary in our small town. And for the next 18 years, I barely missed a service. Sunday morning. Sunday night. Wednesday evening.

But if I'm honest, it felt more like religion than true faith, more like an obligation than an ongoing conversation in our household about God. Going to church every time the doors were open and carving out time to serve in some capacity were things I *had* to do to get to heaven.

Once, a family member told me that when I got to heaven, there'd be a big book with my name in it. Under my name, I'd see a list of all the things I'd ever done wrong in my life, and I'd have to explain why I'd done them. So of course, I associated God with a need to "be perfect" or else I'd be punished.

Let me tell you, instilling that kind of fear will mess with a kid. I thought I'd never be good enough, but *dammit,* I sure was going to try my hardest to reach these impossible standards. I did everything I could to earn love, stay in line, and outrun that list I was growing longer by the day.

Looking back, there's a lot about growing up in church that I appreciate. I'm grateful that I grew up knowing God was my Creator. I'm glad I learned to be a good person, hold values of kindness and loyalty, and take care of others. I'm proud to have learned all the Bible stories in Sunday school. But I can see that what I developed through those experiences wasn't faith. True faith is believing in something you can't see—not breaking yourself down to be "good enough."

There's a Bible school song about a wise man who built his house on a solid rock foundation and a foolish man who built his on sand. When it rained and flooded, the house on the rock stood firm, while the foolish man's house fell apart. If I look at my faith that way, I'd say my foundation is somewhere between rock and sand. There are some seams in the sheetrock that don't line up perfectly. Some cracks in the walls. But the house is still standing.

Many of us were given religion before we could develop a relationship with God. If your earliest memories around faith come with guilt, shame, or fear, you're not the only one trying to sort out what's worth keeping and what's not.

But your faith, whatever it is, is the foundation of your entire life. It's OK to reevaluate the faith you inherited. It's OK to ask yourself: *Did I ever believe this? Or was I just trying to be good enough?*

Maybe your foundation has cracks like mine. Maybe you've had doubts or seasons where you've run away from your faith altogether. But if you're still wondering what a solid faith you can lean on might feel like, then your house is still standing too. Why not choose now to take a peek inside?

The Doubting Years

To understand how I arrived at my current faith, I need to show how much I tried to abandon it earlier in life. I spent my college years trying to run from God. The funny thing was, I went to a Christian college and had to take a Bible class every semester. One day, I was sitting in my Great Christian Doctrine class about teaching others and bringing them to Christ. I couldn't stop the doubts from rising up in me any longer. My mind kept telling me God wasn't real, that none of it was. After that class, I went to meet with the professor in his office.

I sat down and started sobbing.

"I can't tell others about Christ. I don't even believe any of this myself."

It was devastating to feel this way. My whole life, I'd been taught what to believe. Why couldn't I just *believe* it?

That sweet professor could have shamed me, but he didn't. He hugged me and said, "I appreciate you coming in and sharing this with me. I'm proud of you for being honest about your feelings."

He said that he wanted me to come back and see him when I found my faith. Which I would do three years later with something real to share.

It's OK to admit your doubts. Be honest with yourself first. Then confide in someone you trust. If it doesn't happen right away, these conversations can still put you on a path toward the belief system that's always been there, waiting for you to find it. I'll never forget how

> **IT'S OK TO ADMIT YOUR DOUBTS. BE HONEST WITH YOURSELF FIRST. THEN CONFIDE IN SOMEONE YOU TRUST.**

that professor met my doubts with compassion instead of correction. It showed me what grace could look like in real life.

The Dream That Changed Everything

Years later, my doubts hadn't disappeared, but then something happened that I couldn't explain away. To be honest with you, I'm not sure how I feel about visions or "hearing" the voice of God. But I can tell you about a personal experience that changed my life.

About five years into that season of wrestling with my faith, God came to me while I was sleeping one night. In the dream, I was walking through a massive, bright room. I was disoriented, but I had this sense that God was there. He was pretty angry with me.

He asked, "Robin, what are you doing? Why are you doing this to yourself? Do you really believe your mistakes can keep me from loving you?"

He then walked me into what looked like a baby's nursery. He pointed to three beds and said, "They are right here with me."

Instantly, I knew those beds were for each of the babies I had aborted when I was younger. He continued, "Do you think I didn't know what you would do? Do you think I was surprised that you made those choices?"

He looked at me and said, "Why do you think I sent my Son? Why do you think I had to make the ultimate sacrifice? I had to give up my own Son so that all of your sins would be forgiven. I know heartbreak. Don't worry, they are safe here with me."

In the dream, I fell to the ground weeping.

I said to Him, "But killing my own babies…that is unforgivable, it has to be."

He replied, "Please, don't say that. Are you telling me that my Son dying for you wasn't good enough for you?"

I looked up at Him and said, "What? Of course your Son is good enough for me. He is too good for me."

That's when God took on an angry "dad" voice.

"Then stop it. Stop saying that I'm not real. Stop saying that my Son isn't real. Stop acting like you are better than Jesus."

I jolted awake with my heart racing and my mind clearer than it had ever been.

When I woke up, I knew something in me had changed. That moment helped me find faith. I learned you're never too far gone to find the right path again. Your faith is the rock you lean on in your darkest moments. You nurture it daily because you *need* it to hold you up, so you don't fall apart. For years, I used my pain as punishment, trying to outrun grace instead of receiving it. Now, I knew I was worthy of leaning on Him for support.

The day after I had that dream, I went to church and walked to the front of the room for the altar call when the preacher asked if anyone wanted to come forward to ask for forgiveness and prayer. That was the day I truly accepted Jesus as my Savior.

I wish I could say I put my trust in the Lord and everything was roses from that point forward. It wasn't. I would go on to make thousands of mistakes. Things would get even uglier for me before they got better. My faith would get rocked again ten years later. But from that day forward, I never again felt alone. I knew God was real, and I needed Him in my life. I had found my faith; grace would take longer. That came years later in the most unexpected way.

Grace That Just Won't Quit

In 2003, after my first divorce, I ran into an old friend at the grocery store. She was someone I'd gone to church with when I was still married. I had since stopped going. At the time, church didn't feel like a safe place for a divorced woman who'd had an affair.

Naturally, the topic of church came up, and her eyes lit up, "Oh my gosh, Robin, we're going to this new church and you've *got* to come."

I thought about it for a minute. "You know, I really should. I miss that part of my life."

The following Sunday, I went to my friend's church and cried throughout the entire service. It was a nondenominational church, and the preacher spoke about love, grace, and forgiveness in an affirming way that I'd never experienced before.

The church I grew up in had ingrained in me such a deep belief that if I wasn't perfect, I'd go to hell. Since I wasn't perfect, and I felt so broken, I didn't think I belonged in church at all.

But from that day at my new church, I started to understand the difference between religion and *relationship*. I didn't have to strive for perfection or "earn" anything. I knew I was already loved.

I went back to that church every week and cried every time. About a decade later, after I'd become good friends with the pastor and his wife, we laughed about it together.

They said, "We used to watch you every week. You cried every Sunday for years!"

I laughed, "I know! I just couldn't believe it. Y'all told me I wasn't broken. You told me He loved me anyway. I had never heard that before. When you've been so hurt and suddenly feel so loved, it's a lot to process emotionally."

Back in college, my dream helped me *know* God's love. But wiping away tears in those pews at my new church every Sunday, I started to truly *believe* that there was nothing I could do to make God love me less. There was nothing I needed to do to "deserve it." God's love was a gift. All I had to do was accept it, and He would help me rebuild my life from there. Accepting grace was one thing, but learning to live like I believed it took time.

Faith in Real Life

Once I finally stopped trying to "do faith" right and started treating it like a relationship, a real shift began in me. It was a gradual, layer-by-layer process, like peeling an onion. From 2003 to 2015, God kept gently exposing the things I'd buried, tried to run from, or perform my way out of. But it didn't feel like a punishment; it felt like slowly being set free.

Up to that point, I'd built my life around the voice in my head that said, "Robin, do more." But now I could see that "more" wasn't feasible and isn't what God wants for us anyway.

God offers peace, joy, kindness, goodness, mercy—all these things—because He wants us to have a restful life. Not a strife-filled life. Maybe I see that more clearly now because I'm older and more mature. It could be that I've eased up on my drive to perform because time has allowed me to see that life isn't all about *me*.

Whatever it is, I know that this healing process God walked me through has allowed me to show up how I want to in the world and love others unconditionally. Whether that's a coworker I'm mentoring, a young girl navigating postabortion grief, or my children, I can pour into them because of everything God has poured into me.

I recently heard Jelly Roll share how God turned his life around, from addiction and jail to music and ministry. He's open about his past as a former drug dealer and addict who's been arrested multiple times. His life was horrific, and then he found God. His story reminded me that redemption is always possible. You can't explain that kind of transformation without faith.

Stories like mine, Jelly Roll's, and many others are why I know God is real. I've done life without Him and I've done life with Him, and let me tell you, you want to be in His boat. My life is so good now, and I still feel God giving me nudges to stay the course all the time.

My husband's fishing club does dinners on Friday nights, and my work schedule typically doesn't allow me to go. But right before I started writing this chapter, I was free one Friday night, so we went together.

The man running the event called me out, "Shannon's wife, Robin, is here tonight. It's so great to have her. And by the way, she's writing a book!"

Everyone in the room turned to me, and he continued, "I don't want to put her on the spot, but you should know, Robin, we're all going to want to buy a copy of that book."

Later that evening, other wives came up to me with questions about the book. They wanted to know the title, what it was about, and which stories I'd share.

I said, "Well, it touches on everything. The family you were born into, the family you create, your job, your mother, your faith, your pain. Pretty much everything that makes us women."

"Oh wow, we can't wait!"

See, I believe that was God putting people on my path to affirm my decision to write this book. Writing a book is a huge project. It gives you a lot of time sitting with the voice in your head that will sometimes say, "This is stupid. Nobody's going to care about this."

But every time I need a shot in the arm, I have a moment like that where I feel God whisper, "Those thoughts aren't true. Keep going. Don't stop. Don't lose your fire for this."

> BUT EVERY TIME I NEED A SHOT IN THE ARM, I HAVE A MOMENT LIKE THAT WHERE I FEEL GOD WHISPER, "THOSE THOUGHTS AREN'T TRUE. KEEP GOING. DON'T STOP. DON'T LOSE YOUR FIRE FOR THIS."

You can't know everything, and that's why it's called faith. But after all these years, all the missteps, tears, and transformation I've gone through, I do know God's love for me is unwavering, and my belief in Him is too.

What I Know for Sure

I don't know the technical differences between faith, spirituality, and religion. But as I made my way through life, I learned there were things I could not explain with logic. You can be handed one religion or belief system, but the strongest faith is the one you build for yourself. Through my journey with faith, I know in my bones that God is real. His spirit lives in me. I can feel his presence and guidance. It's the small voice that tells me when something's not right.

My God is a good Father, and He loves me more than I can ever imagine. I get the sense that when He looks down on me, He's proud of me. I know that's a crazy thing to believe. But it feels as real to me as this keyboard I'm typing on.

How could a Father love his daughter when she's messed up as much as I have? I've broken all of the Ten Commandments. I put my faith in things other than God, like money, status, and finances. I've told lies. I've committed adultery.

But then I think about how much I love my own kids. Is there anything they could ever do that would make me stop loving them? No. They can break my heart a million times, and I still love them. Associating God with a parental figure feels like the most natural comparison.

I once heard someone explain that faith is only about two things:

1. Belief in God
2. Belief that God will always do what He says He will do.

It seems so simple, but finding your faith and letting it guide you is the hardest, most beautiful thing you'll ever do.

Finding Your People and Your Peace

If you're at rock bottom, what I want to tell you is to find a good church, like the one I cried in every Sunday for a decade. But more than anything, I'd say to find a good, healthy, loving community. You can't do it all alone.

There's so much church hurt out there. So many people have been hurt by judgmental, religious crap. I wish someone had told me sooner that it doesn't have to be what faith means to you. You don't have to give up on God because of a bad church experience. If you want to know God, call out to Him. All you have to do is say, "Lord, I need you." And he'll be there. It's that simple.

Having faith doesn't mean having a perfect life. That doesn't exist.

> **IF YOU WANT TO KNOW GOD, CALL OUT TO HIM. ALL YOU HAVE TO DO IS SAY, "LORD, I NEED YOU." AND HE'LL BE THERE. IT'S THAT SIMPLE.**

But when the floods come—and they will come—you want your house built on rock. You want a solid, steady presence in the boat with you. And the wildest thing is, the creator of the waves themselves is willing to ride it out with you.

Whatever your beliefs are, I think most of us, especially women, need something to hold on to when life gets too heavy. We're expected to be everything: strong yet soft, ambitious yet selfless, polished yet never too much. We carry guilt for wanting more and shame for not being enough.

I think it's important for us to have a belief system that reminds us that none of that changes our worth. You don't have to earn love, perform for peace, or prove you're good enough to be here. I hope you find whatever does that for you, whether it's in a church service, in a dream, or in a supportive group of girlfriends. Find a foundation that can hold you steady when everything goes sideways.

You don't have to be perfect. You're not too far gone, and you're not alone. You're still here, and your house is still standing for the day you're ready to return home.

CHAPTER 10

Physical Health, Aging, and Listening to Your Body

We waste good health on our youth,
then spend our golden years chasing it.

For most of my life, I didn't think twice about my physical health. I could outrun exhaustion and outwork stress. I was the gal who'd put in 60-hour weeks at my job, went home and took four kids to their after-school activities, put home-cooked meals on the table, folded laundry, and then woke up to do it all again the next day.

But in my mid-40s, I slammed into a brick wall. I was constantly exhausted, unfocused, and I couldn't lose weight no matter what I tried. It felt like I woke up and wasn't Robin anymore.

In a way, I guess I'm lucky that my body waited that long to start saying "no." But when it did, it was so dang loud! My mind tried to tell my body to shut up and perform like it always had.

But for the first time in my life, my body didn't obey. Instead, it barked back, "I don't think so."

That's the thing about physical health—many of us don't think about it until we have to.

It makes me laugh thinking about how I used to neglect my body. I assumed it'd always be able to operate at the same speed it did in my 20s. That's like not thinking about retirement until it's time to retire. (In chapter 11, we'll talk about why *that's* not a good idea either.)

You shouldn't wait to take care of your body until it screams at you. It doesn't matter if you're younger or much older than your mid-40s. This chapter is here to remind you to listen for your body's whispers, so it doesn't have to get angry to get your attention.

As women, we all have seasons where we feel like we're losing it. Maybe it's snapping at your kids for something small, then crying in the pantry five minutes later because you don't know why you're upset. Maybe you have brain fog or chronic fatigue, and your doctors won't listen. You can choose to gaslight yourself and see these symptoms as personal failings. But instead, what if you got curious about what your body is trying to say?

One of those days when I couldn't get myself up off the couch, I looked up at my husband, Shannon, with tears in my eyes and asked, "What's wrong with me?"

ONE OF THOSE DAYS WHEN I COULDN'T GET MYSELF UP OFF THE COUCH, I LOOKED UP AT MY HUSBAND, SHANNON, WITH TEARS IN MY EYES AND ASKED, "WHAT'S WRONG WITH ME?"

He looked at me with concern, and for the first time, we discussed whether I was experiencing a deeper health issue that needed to be addressed. That's when I started digging for answers I didn't even know I needed. I didn't know it at the time, but my body wasn't broken. It was just trying to tell me something no one had taught me to listen for.

That was the first moment that I thought maybe I *wasn't* going crazy. Maybe there was more going on here. That's when I started digging for answers I didn't know I needed. I learned later that my body wasn't broken. It was just trying to tell me something no one had taught me to listen for.

The "Mysteries" of the Female Body

After listening to hundreds of podcasts and seeing multiple doctors, I now know that the brick wall I hit was perimenopause. I didn't know that I had actually been in this season of life since my 30s.

Today, I'm glad to see more women talking openly about menopause and its many symptoms because it's so much more than night sweats (which I never got). Here are a few ways perimenopause showed up for me:

- My sleep quality plummeted.
- I couldn't focus on work for more than two hours at a time.
- I couldn't make it through the workday without needing a nap.
- My hair was starting to fall out, and my skin was dry as a bone.

- I cut carbs, ate good protein, walked five miles a day, yet couldn't lose weight.

No one told me symptoms like this could be linked to hormonal changes, so I felt lost. At one point, I got so frustrated by the new way my body was behaving that I decided to do an experiment. I ate nothing except chicken broth, black coffee, and water for seven days. I lost one pound. That's when I said, "Screw it." Thanksgiving was coming up, so I decided to eat whatever I wanted for seven days: slices of pumpkin pie with vanilla ice cream, second helpings of sweet potato casserole—the works.

After that holiday week, I couldn't believe what I saw when I stepped on the scale: I had only gained one pound. My weight wasn't going down, but it wasn't going up either.

This wasn't normal for me, so I figured something in my body must have shut down. I didn't know what that meant yet, but it didn't seem good. Several medical professionals didn't know what to do with me either. The first few doctors I saw didn't suggest that I might be entering perimenopause. They didn't bring up hormones at all.

As it turns out, there's a reason so many women leave the doctor's office feeling unheard. The clinical studies that help the medical field learn more about human health didn't include women until recently. Trials and testing only started bringing in female participants in the late 1980s, and including us didn't become mandatory until 1993.[5] No wonder the healthcare

---

5 Khanna, Deeptha. "Women's health: Why is the health of at least half the global population so often overlooked?" *World Economic Forum*, January 2, 2023, https://www.weforum.org/stories/2023/01/women-health-gap-davos-2023/.

system is still catching up when it comes to understanding our bodies.

When I did more research on women's health, I found Dr. Mary Claire Haver, an OB/GYN from Texas. In her books, Dr. Haver talks about how little she learned about menopause in her medical training.[6] She thought the women she treated were just being "women." Then, she entered perimenopause herself. She became embarrassed about the things she used to say to women in her care, and how wrong she now knew those comments were. (Talk about a *real* doctor who's woman enough to admit when she's wrong!)

It made me feel seen for a doctor to admit she hadn't gotten the information she needed to help someone like me. Learning from knowledgeable medical professionals like Dr. Haver helped me finally see my perimenopause for what it was. By 46, I was in full-blown menopause, meaning I didn't have periods at all anymore. I still didn't know how to start feeling better. At least now I had language for what was happening.

It's so important for women to talk about our health not only with our doctors, but also with our friends, daughters, and mothers. The more we know about what other women go through and the issues members of our family have experienced—and not only with perimenopause—the better we're able to take care of ourselves.

---

6 Mary Claire Haver, *The New Menopause: Navigating Your Path Through Hormonal Change with Purpose, Power, and Facts* (New York: Rodale Books, 2024).

Know Your Family History Before It Repeats Itself

We grow up aware of the more obvious health issues in our families. For example, my grandma had multiple sclerosis for over 40 years. She was paralyzed from the neck down with only the use of her hands, and she had to be carried to and from a wheelchair. We, her family, had to do everything from giving her baths to catheterizing her.

But much of your family's health history may go unsaid until you need to know. Maybe an intake form asks if there's any history of a specific condition in your family, so you have to call up someone you can ask. Or maybe you only find out when you start showing signs of something that runs in the family.

That happened to me in adulthood. My ears started to feel like I was in an airplane and couldn't get them to pop. I had several appointments at the ENT (ear, nose, and throat) doctor and couldn't figure out what was going on. But when I complained to my mom, she told me she had a hereditary, degenerative condition called otosclerosis that affects the ear canal, so it must run in our family. *Thanks, Mom!*

Your lineage probably has more answers for your health issues than you realize and some are even more vital to know. My dad had a massive heart attack at 45 and had open-heart quadruple bypass surgery. My uncles and aunt on his side all had heart attacks too. When I developed pneumonia a few years ago, I had my family's cardiovascular issues at the back of my mind.

The radiologist did an X-ray of my lungs and then handed it off to my pulmonologist, who put it up on a screen for us to look at together. We talked for a few minutes, then my eyes fixated on a note at the bottom of the radiology report that no one had brought to my attention. It said something about significant calcification in my arteries.

My heart started racing. They were looking for issues in my lungs, but why hadn't anyone mentioned this detail to me? I was the only one in that clinic who knew the extent of my family's history with heart conditions. I was the only one who knew how urgent that note was.

If you're young, you may not see the need to be aware of your family's health history. But by the time you're in your 50s, you really need to know about these details because they'll start affecting your life more directly. And by then, you may not have as many family members you can ask. So don't wait for a crisis. Reach out now to learn what you can about your family's health.

Once you know what you're working with, you're in a better position to manage your health. You don't have to guess. You can trust yourself more to make informed decisions about the kind of care your body actually needs.

Trusting Your Gut

Growing up, I watched my grandma take pill after pill to manage her multiple sclerosis. One pill treated a symptom, a second pill offset the side effects of the first, and so on. This history set my mom on alternative paths of healing in the early 1980s, and she came to see medicine as the very last resort.

I love that I learned this approach from my mom. Many years later, my kids would joke that I never took them to the doctor, and they were right most of the time. My personal belief is that if we leave our bodies alone, they'll ultimately heal themselves. Until they don't. Then and only then do we need to put something in our bodies.

After that note at the pulmonologist's office sent me into a panic, I met with a cardiologist whose advice was to lose weight, exercise, and start taking a cholesterol medication.

"It feels like every doctor I speak to wants to make me go away with one pill or another, rather than getting to the root of the problem," I said to my chiropractor after updating her on the whole situation.

That's when my chiropractor told me about a doctor who was doing some innovative work in the area of heart health. This doctor was the picture of health as a marathon runner, triathlete, you name it. And he had a massive heart attack at 48 years old. Since he'd dealt with these issues himself and shared my preference for avoiding prescriptions unless completely necessary, I decided to book an appointment.

When we met, we discussed the calcification in my arteries, but I made sure to tell him the whole picture of my health. My exhaustion. My sleep issues. The Thanksgiving experiment.

"Ah," the doctor said, "Menopause."

Finally, I was in the room with a medical professional who was on the same page as me. And not only that, he immediately saw issues with my other doctors' recommendations. The medication my cardiologist wanted to put me on? That would've exacerbated my hormonal brain fog and fatigue.

So instead of going the medical route, my new doctor put me on a monthslong detox regimen. We worked on gut health with a cleanse, an elimination diet, and food testing. I discovered foods I didn't know I was allergic to, learned I had a leaky gut, and took steps to heal it. We did blood work to figure out what was going on with my body on a cellular level. And we focused on balancing my hormones and improving my heart health.

Through this work, I've lost 50 pounds, and I feel younger than I did when my menopause began. In my late 40s, I looked old! I had so much inflammation in my body, and I could see it in the photos we took at the start of my treatment. My skin looked dull and lifeless, and I looked *exhausted*. Now, I'm stronger, I have more energy, and I'm enjoying my life again.

All because I trusted my intuition.

I didn't settle for one doctor's decision to write a prescription on the first visit. I tell you to do the same: don't settle when it comes to something as important as your health. Fight for your body and your right to feel good in it. Love your body like it's going to carry you another 40 years because if you're lucky, it will.

> **LOVE YOUR BODY LIKE IT'S GOING TO CARRY YOU ANOTHER 40 YEARS BECAUSE IF YOU'RE LUCKY, IT WILL.**

Befriending Your Body

The process of healing my body wasn't easy, but I'd do it all again. When your health starts to go, you realize that feeling good in your body is essential to experiencing joy, clarity, confidence, and control in every area of your life.

Most of the women in my generation spent our younger years treating our bodies like they were indestructible. We slept in our makeup, laid out in the sun slathered in baby oil, and ate fast food like it was fuel. We drank like fish, ran on fumes, and figured our bodies would bounce back no matter what we put them through.

But if you live like that, one day you wake up and realize that you no longer recognize the person in the mirror. The weight doesn't budge. The energy's gone. Your skin looks dull, and your brain feels fuzzy. You start to wonder if this is how it's going to be from now on. That's your body whispering, "Hey, we can't live like this anymore."

When you ignore those whispers, they get louder. For me, a little grogginess became an inability to stay awake. A stubborn ten pounds turned into my body shutting down. And a hunch around my family's heart health could have led to a serious cardiac event if I hadn't intervened.

That's the whole point, isn't it? We shouldn't take care of our bodies to avoid disaster or to try to look 30 forever. For me, maintaining good health is about doing the things I love for years to come. It means having enough energy to hike the hills, dance at weddings, or run with my grandbabies through the sprinklers.

So I'm not focused on eternal youth. I'm working toward getting stronger rather than skinnier. I'm focused on keeping my energy up rather than expecting myself to run on fumes.

I exercise and eat well because I want to feel good and keep showing up for my people, not because I want to punish myself.

You have to define what the best relationship with *your* body feels like. It's different for each of us. But here's an invitation, if you're up for it.

Repeat after me:

> I love my body.
>
> I'm going to move my body so I can be strong, not skinny.
>
> I'm going to take care of my body.
>
> My body is going to take care of me.
>
> My body is beautiful.
>
> I'm going to feed my body beautiful, healthy foods…and the occasional treat.

Aging happens to the luckiest among us, but it can feel like a punishment when we don't take care of ourselves. Don't wait until you feel like the walking dead to improve your relationship with the vehicle that carries you through this life. Your actions today can improve how you feel in your body tomorrow.

What's one healthy habit your future self will thank you for starting now?

CHAPTER 11

Financial Health

I don't love money, but I sure love the options it provides.

L et's be honest. For most of us, money is a sensitive subject. If you're like me, it's something you wish you'd figured out way earlier in life. We've all made at least one embarrassing money decision, like blowing a paycheck on something ridiculous or treating our savings account like a revolving door.

You may be inclined to skip this chapter because it's not fun to talk about something so stressful. Please don't. I wish someone had sat me down decades ago and told me the real value of money; it gives you options in life.

A secure financial situation means you can change jobs if you need to. You can leave a bad relationship if you need to. You can take care of your family if a sudden emergency comes up. You can retire when you want to. (If you're 25, I'm sure that feels like a lifetime away. But I can tell you at 53, my 25th birthday feels like yesterday!)

The point is, money gives you choices, and that's a nice perk. You will literally have less tension in your body, better mental health, and a less frazzled nervous system when you know that if shit hits the fan, you'll be OK.

Most of us don't have perfect money habits, and who can blame us? We aren't taught money skills in school, and many of us have harmful attitudes about money passed down from our parents.

But imagine how powerful it'd be if we all released the negative financial beliefs that hold us back, learned what we need to give ourselves options, and helped other women get a leg up in this area that we don't talk about enough.

As much as you can, go into this exploration without shame or judgment. Even if things haven't always gone the way you wanted them to, the insights you uncover can help you navigate financial decisions with more confidence and clarity.

The Emotional Side of Money

We spend most of our waking lives earning money, spending it, saving it (or not), and stressing over it. We work for money in one way or another, yet many of us never really learn how to make money work for us.

As a little girl growing up in the South, I quickly learned the three topics you're *never* supposed to discuss: politics, religion, and money. Bringing up any of these topics could get you side-eyed at the dinner table, but money always felt the most off-limits. It was rude to bring it up, tacky to flaunt it, and shameful to admit you didn't have enough.

When you're raised to tiptoe around money, it starts to feel like something to fear or avoid. But when we avoid something as important as money, we don't allow ourselves to get better at managing it. Instead, often without realizing it, we may start to form unhelpful beliefs about wealth, scarcity, and what it means to be "good" with money. The truth is, money isn't only about the number on your bank statement. It's about choices, security, and peace of mind. For many of us, money is seriously emotional!

Today, I am very aware of how lucky I am that I don't have to stand at the grocery store checkout and do quick math to be sure I have enough to cover the total. I've seen a mom, more than once, standing ahead of me in line, watching the dollar amounts ring up on the screen. She has the generic store brand of everything, and she's buying bread, peanut butter, rice, beans, hamburger meat, and only canned vegetables.

You can tell she's doing her very best to stretch that dollar.

She moves items from the front of the conveyor belt to the back until ultimately, she has to hand the last-priority items to the cashier and tell her to please put them back.

When I see this happen, it feels like I was put there at that exact time and day to fill the gap for her. I love being able to make eye contact with the cashier and tell her, "Add those items back. I've got the difference."

The mom turns and looks at me, sometimes mouthing the words "thank you" and other times just a smile and a nod.

It makes me cry thinking about those times. For me, money has always carried an emotional weight. I know what it's like to grow up between the extremes of having plenty and having very little.

A Surprising Aspect of the Financial Rollercoaster

When my mom was married to my stepdad, his business was thriving and there was plenty of money to go around. On the outside, things looked great: nice clothes, a big house, and a solid sense that we had "enough." But behind closed doors, life didn't feel stable.

Remember in chapter 3 when I told you about my stepdad throwing our Christmas tree through the living room? Same guy. My stepdad was controlling and abusive when I was a child and when things got bad, my mom and I would pack up and move out to live on our own. Leaving him and going back was a pattern we repeated for a while.

What's interesting, though, is that you'd think more money would mean more peace of mind, and less money would mean more stress, but that's not what my childhood taught me.

The instability I experienced when we lived with my stepdad caused me to associate having a lot of money with more stress and chaos. For a while, I subconsciously believed that wealth and stress went hand in hand. I had the mindset: *If you have a lot of money, get ready, because you're in for some tumultuous times. And is that really worth it?*

On the other hand, during those bouts of living away from my stepdad, we didn't have much money. But life was simpler, and I associated less money with more safety and emotional security.

This is the tricky, psychological aspect of money that can trip you up and cause you to develop bad financial habits. I could have made decisions in life that caused me to keep struggling since subconsciously my brain was wired to see money as a threat. But luckily, I've developed an awareness of the role money plays in my world. Now I'm determined to not allow money to be the primary driver of happiness in my life.

It took me years to unlearn the belief that financial success comes with emotional turmoil. But once I did, I realized a simple truth: Security comes from your relationship with money, not how much you have.

The Power of Giving

During those seasons of having very little, I would get so mad at my mom because she would put a check on the plate at church every Sunday. Meanwhile, I was over there thinking, *You're a single mom. We have no money! Surely God will understand!*

But when I got upset with her she said, "Robin, I don't care if I have one dollar or one thousand dollars. I always give."

I get emotional thinking about how grateful I am that her attitude was seeded in me from a young age. In adulthood, I started living that practice myself, and I believe it's a big part of why I've been blessed financially in my life.

The Bible tells us to give 10% of what we earn and that's the "rule." That's what my mom did, so when I started working,

I did the same. But in my 30s, I heard a lesson about it being impossible to outgive God. We were told that this is something God wants us to "test" Him on. So, I decided to try it. I made a deal with God that I'd continue giving my 10%, but I'd also give until I felt it—until there was a sacrifice.

As a commission-earning salesperson, it was very easy to see how this played out. For example, I sold $300,000 and earned a commission, so I gave 10% and then listened to the "extra" number I was supposed to give. Sometimes, I'd hear 25% more, so I did it. Then, the next deal I worked on was $1M. When I earned a commission on that, same thing. I gave 10% and then listened for the extra number.

God and I played this game all the way up to a BILLION-dollar deal. I tried to outgive Him and He continued to outgive me right back. It was such a fun way to live and give. It truly is so much better to give than to receive.

My advice to younger Robin would be to try to see money as a tool you can use to make your world better, rather than a burden. Live life with your hands open, so you can receive more and bless others. When you lead with abundance instead of fear, money might come back to you in ways you don't expect.

What School Didn't Teach You About Money

Many people feel uncertainty around money. The best way to gain confidence is to take action. Let's bust some common money myths and explore simple actions you can take for more financial security.

I'll preface this by saying that **I am not a financial or investment advisor**. None of this is professional financial advice nor is it a full picture of how you should manage your finances. These are bits of wisdom I've picked up along the way as food for thought. This is stuff I wish someone had opened my eyes to earlier on in life.

Also laws and specific dollar amounts change regularly. These numbers were accurate to the best of my knowledge at the time of this writing, but please consult a professional and look into these things independently to find the right path for you.

You wouldn't go your whole life without seeing a doctor. So why go your whole life without seeing a financial advisor?

Money Myth #1: A 401(k) Is All You Need for Retirement

For a long time, I thought maxing out my 401(k) with the companies I've worked with meant I was set for retirement. I was doing everything I was "supposed" to do. But the day I ran the numbers, I almost choked on my coffee.

Here I am in my 50s. I've made six figures for 30 years, and I can't retire yet and maintain the lifestyle I'm accustomed to. I didn't know that my 401(k) alone wouldn't be enough to retire early. It's better than nothing but not enough. There are other avenues and investments I could have made when I was younger, if only I'd known!

Action Step: If your company offers a 401(k) match, contribute up to that amount. Beyond that, put any additional retirement savings into more flexible investments. That way you can access them sooner than the traditional retirement age if needed. (Consult a tax professional to determine what approach makes the most sense for your individual situation.)

Advanced Tip: Your retirement accounts and stock holdings aren't just for saving. You can leverage them to grow your wealth in other ways. For example, if I wanted to purchase property, I could borrow against my 401(k), retirement savings, and stock portfolio rather than taking out a bank loan for the full amount.

A financial advisor just taught me that in my 50s, dad-gummit! He said, "The wealthy don't just save. They use money to make money."

Money Myth #2: Talking About Money Is Rude

If, like me, you grew up believing that discussing money was impolite, you probably didn't learn enough to build good money habits in adulthood. Wealthy people talk about money frequently, and guess what? They keep getting wealthier because they:

- Share financial knowledge
- Get expert advice on their money situation
- Learn saving and investment strategies from peers
- Make the most of tax advantages and business ventures

- Normalize conversations around salaries and building wealth

Silence around money is why so many people stay stuck. Women in particular are often left out of these conversations, which means we miss out on opportunities to gain financial wisdom, develop a better relationship with money, and grow our wealth to its fullest potential. Sometimes I wonder why my daughter and I have similar behaviors around money, while my sons have a totally different financial outlook.

My 24-year-old son Carter is maxing out five or six different investment accounts and calculating the savings he needs to buy a home with his new wife soon. My 18- and 19-year-old sons, Graham and Spencer, took their high school graduation money and started investment accounts. They figure that if they leave that money alone in an actively traded account, they'll be millionaires by 38.

Why didn't I learn these lessons my sons have already applied to their lives? To me, it feels like women often assume that being "good with money" means being thrifty, keeping a budget, and saving, while men are taught that being "good" with money means building wealth and investing.

I'm not sure why that is, but I'd love to see the narrative shift. Nothing sounds more badass to me than opening the dialogue for women to talk about this stuff so we can help each other grow our wealth.

Action Step: Start talking about money with people you trust. Ask a financially savvy friend how they invest or open up a conversation about salary with colleagues. You could read a personal finance book and share what you learn at the dinner table with your partner or kids. The more you know, the better decisions you can make.

Advanced Tip: Find a mentor or financial advisor and have an intentional conversation about financial strategies.

And remember, if you have a negative experience with a financial advisor, keep talking! You're interviewing them, not the other way around. Keep going until you find someone who listens, explains things clearly, and cares about your goals.

Money Myth #3: Your Lifestyle Should Match Your Total Household Income

Some households do need two incomes to stay afloat, especially in today's world. But when I was growing up, my nanny always told me, "You need to be able to live on one income and save the second income."

Looking back now, I can see how that was such smart advice! I wish I'd taken it. If you can structure your lifestyle around one paycheck, you can create extra financial breathing room by saving or investing as much of the other income as possible.

I won't lie, this takes discipline. But I've seen firsthand how families who build their budget around one income and invest the other set themselves up for stability and long-term wealth.

Action Step: Take a hard look at your finances and see where you could live on less. Even if you can't survive on one income, start saving a bigger percentage of what you bring in as a household. Invest it, use it to pay off debt, or build an emergency fund.

Advanced Tip: If your kids have earned income, consider putting it into a custodial Roth IRA. Only $100/month invested from birth could become significant wealth by the time they're ready to retire. This is an incredibly simple way to set your family up for generational abundance.

The Big Picture: How Time and Money Work Together

The sooner you start saving for retirement, the longer you have to take advantage of the power of compound interest. Unlike money sitting in a typical bank account with minimal growth, compound interest lets you earn returns on both your initial investment and the interest it earns over time. This helps your wealth multiply faster, so it's easier to reach financial goals like retiring when and how you want to.

Here's an approximate breakdown of how much you need to save monthly to hit $1 million by retirement. The numbers here assume an 8% average return, but returns generally vary between 6% and 10%. Starting earlier means you end up with more and have to invest less of your own money overall.

Age you start	Monthly investment	Total contributed	Total at age 60
20	$350	$160,000	$1M
30	$800	$288,000	$1.2M
40	$2,200	$528,000	$1.3M
50	$8,000	$960,000	$1.4M

Smart Money Moves for Your Kids and Grandkids

Saving for college: If you start investing into a 529 plan when your child is born, you'll have more than enough money to pay for their college by the time they turn 18. If they don't use it all, you can transfer leftover funds into a Roth IRA for their retirement under certain conditions.

Put them on payroll: If you have a business, you can legally pay your child up to $14,600 per year (in 2025) for legitimate work (think product modeling or administrative tasks), and it's tax-free. This earned income can also be invested in a Roth IRA up to the annual limit.

Help kids build credit early: Make your kids authorized users on your credit cards. This will make it easier for them to qualify for their own loans and credit cards later, and hopefully they won't need you to cosign.

Smart gifting: You can gift up to $19,000 per year to a UGMA/UTMA brokerage account without reporting to the IRS (Internal Revenue Service) or paying a gift tax. That means if both parents contribute, that's $38,000 a year toward their future!

Invest on behalf of your grandkids: If you gift $36,000 ($18,000 per grandparent) in low-cost index funds inside a custodial brokerage account for a grandchild, that money could grow to $10.9 million by the time they're 59 if left untouched (assuming an 8% average return). Talk about a financial game-changer.

It's Never Too Early or Too Late

My biggest message for you is that it's never too late to improve your financial situation. But if you're young, start now! It doesn't have to be overwhelming, and you don't need thousands of dollars to invest. You just have to start somewhere.

If I've learned anything over the years, it's that wealth sure as hell doesn't happen by accident. It's an intentional relationship you have to build and tend to over time.

This isn't about how much money you have today. It's about what you do with it. When you use your resources to care for yourself, support your people, give generously, and build the kind of life you actually want, money goes from stressful to powerful.

PART 3 REFLECTION:
TIME TO GET REAL

Before you move on, take a moment to pause and reflect on this part of your life. The questions below are here to help you get honest with yourself.

You can journal your answers, talk them out with a friend, or simply sit with them for a bit. But don't be afraid to go deeper than you usually would. Slowing down long enough to really look at your life can help you understand yourself better, make meaningful changes, and become the woman you're meant to be.

1. Where do you feel most emotionally steady, and can you give yourself more credit there? Are you struggling with anything mentally? What would it look like to give yourself the kind of care you offer others?
2. What belief system do you turn to when life feels out of control? Is it still serving you? Is there room to deepen that connection?
3. Is there someone you can ask about your family's health history? Has your body been trying to tell you anything lately? Are you listening?
4. Have you started investing and making smart financial moves for your future? What can you do today to set yourself up better tomorrow?

CONCLUSION

Your Journey Through Fire

There's a Japanese art form called *kintsugi* that I've been thinking about while writing this book. Maybe you've heard of it. It's the practice of taking broken pottery and gluing the pieces back together with a special lacquer that's mixed with gold. The cracks aren't hidden. They're highlighted and celebrated. The new piece of pottery, with its glittering fractures on display, becomes something new and more valuable because of what it survived.

That is a woman's life right there.

We break and we rebuild. We fall apart and rise again. We emerge from unimaginable darkness to face the world with our golden scars radiating in the sunlight of a new day.

Girl by birth, woman by fire.

As women, we don't get out of walking through fire. In some seasons, we may get burned. We may watch our whole lives go up in smoke. But let's talk about what else fire can do.

Take a forest in decline. Not all problems can be solved by fire, but in certain ecosystems, controlled burns can clear undergrowth, recycle nutrients, and make room for new life. In nature, both fire and decay play roles in renewal, each in their own time, creating a forest that can rise greener, healthier, and more alive.

Mold a pot out of clay and paint it red. It doesn't become strong or beautiful until you put it in the kiln and "fire" it. The fire not only makes its color rich. It changes the clay's structure on a molecular level. In a similar way, the hormonal shifts, pressures, and refining processes we endure as women can change us at the core, revealing a deeper strength and vibrance we didn't know we had.

Think about the Bible story of Shadrach, Meshach, and Abednego who were three boys thrown into a fire. Observers watched the fire and saw four people there, not three. Jesus was with them, and when they came out on the other side, they weren't burned. They didn't even smell like smoke.

That's the image I hope you take away from the stories in this book too. I could have walked through the fires of my life—the divorces, abortions, abuse, nervous breakdowns, all of it—and come out on the other side smelling like smoke. I could be bitter. I could still harbor shame. I could have carried anger through the rest of my life.

But I didn't. And that's what I want for you too.

The goal isn't to go through life avoiding the fire. Even the most destructive fires can be catalysts for growth, transformation, and a beautiful life beyond your wildest dreams.

The goal is to come out on the other side without smelling like smoke. And I don't mean to hide your battle wounds. Instead, let the hardships you face bring beauty to your life, like *kintsugi* pottery that becomes better after breaking and being mended.

In this book, I've shared life lessons from the fires I've walked through, some set by others, some sparked by my own choices.

We looked at the relationships in our lives and how they shape our identity, self-worth, and sense of what's possible for our lives. We talked about our careers, the dreams we follow or let go of, and how to keep growing when the path doesn't unfold the way we expected. And we discussed the complex ecosystem of a woman's health: mental, emotional, spiritual, physical, and financial, and what it really means to take care of ourselves.

I hope that through my stories, I've given you a space to reflect on your life and a reminder that your story isn't finished. It's not too late for you to get real with yourself. No matter what you've been through, or what you're going through now, it's never too late to build the life you dream of.

My advice from here? Don't stop doing this work.

Keep naming the patterns you've carried for too long. Keep mending the parts of you that have cracked and broken over the years. Keep asking yourself what you're ready to own and what you're ready to let go of, so you can become the woman you're meant to be.

ABOUT THE AUTHOR

Robin Goad is a proud wife, mother, grandmother, Christian, Texan, and unapologetic truthteller. Over nearly three decades, she built a highly successful corporate career while navigating heartbreak, healing, and the journey back to her most authentic self.

She has led at some of the world's most respected tech companies including Gartner, Dell, and now AWS, where she serves as a technology executive. In the newest chapter of her career, Robin is sharing her hard-won insights as an executive coach and strategic advisor and building a community for the next generation of women leaders. Her focus is helping young professional women understand the unspoken rules of corporate America, identify the unique value they bring to the table, and develop a strategy to excel in their careers.

Named Dell's Working Mother of the Year, featured on CRN's Women of the Channel, and a speaker at high-profile events like SXSW and TEDx, Robin is at home guiding crowds and mentoring women one on one. Outside of work, she loves spending time with her husband, Shannon, her children, Macy, Carter, Graham, and Spencer, and her grandson, James. She never turns down an opportunity to host a houseful of family and friends.

Girl by Birth, Woman by Fire: The Get Real Guide to Becoming the Woman You Were Meant to Be is Robin's first book—a raw and redemptive roadmap rooted in faith, self-discovery, and healing. This book is part of her mission to empower women so they can thrive in their careers and personal lives.